A
T

"Thomas Moore in   e
above the crass c   e
nostalgia of childhood memories. With the eyes of a
mystic and the heart of storyteller, Thomas Moore
explores the ancient myths, archetypal symbols, and
profound images of this holy season. Be ready to gaze
with Moore at the newborn Child and rediscover God's
message to you and to our world."

——RICHARD ROHR, author, teacher, and founder of the
Center for Action and Contemplation

PRAISE FOR THOMAS MOORE

"Thomas Moore has taught us how to discover the holiness concealed in the ordinary."

——RABBI HAROLD S. KUSHNER, author of the bestseller
When Bad Things Happen to Good People

"When [Moore] is read closely, his depth is apparent…he stands to make some new converts to the non-institutional ranks of spirituality."

——*Publishers Weekly*

"Thomas Moore is one of the profound spiritual writers of our time."

——JOHN BRADSHAW, author of the *New York Times*
#1 bestseller *Homecoming*

THE SOUL OF CHRISTMAS

THE
SOUL
OF
CHRISTMAS

THOMAS MOORE

Franciscan
MEDIA
Cincinnati, Ohio

Scripture passages are the author's own translation.

Cover and book design by Mark Sullivan
Cover image © iStock | Borut Trdina

LIBRARY OF CONGRESS CATALOGING-IN-PUBLICATION DATA
Names: Moore, Thomas, 1940- author.
Title: The soul of Christmas / Thomas Moore.
Description: Cincinnati : Franciscan Media, 2016.
Identifiers: LCCN 2016026611 | ISBN 9781632531209 (hard-
cover)
Subjects: LCSH: Christmas. | Jesus Christ—Nativity.
Classification: LCC BV45 .M643 2016 | DDC 242/.335—dc23
LC record available at https://lccn.loc.gov/2016026611

ISBN 978-1-63253-120-9

Published by Franciscan Media
28 W. Liberty St.
Cincinnati, OH 45202
www.FranciscanMedia.org

Printed in the United States of America.
Printed on acid-free paper.
16 17 18 19 20 5 4 3 2 1

Dedicated to Ben and Mary,
Bill and Agnes,
Abe, Ajeet, and Hari Kirin

CONTENTS

A New Day for Spiritual Practices

oday religious observances are going through major changes. One of these is a fresh appreciation for the many spiritual traditions of the world and the relatively new idea that we can benefit from them all without corrupting our individual values. In that spirit, we have a new opportunity now to make Christmas a deeper and more universal celebration of life's promise, thus making the season one of hope for everyone. We can foresee the day when we will exit the usual world of competition and conflict and live by the principle of love.

Personally, I wouldn't write a book on Christmas unless I felt that this holy festival is worth keeping. I wouldn't want to increase any sense of tension among the religions or among atheists and agnostics, all of whom I profoundly respect. But I don't think a culture of secularism is the answer. Ignore Christmas and you lose something precious to your soul.

Today many thoughtful people still reject religion in general when they really mean an old-time form of religion that is intolerant, self-absorbed, moralistic, dogmatic, and sentimental. I have no use for that kind of religiosity either. And yet I am promoting Christmas. I truly believe that we can and should deepen our understanding of Christmas, not to arrive at the "true meaning of Christmas," which usually means some narrow idea of religious exclusivism, but to see how this commemoration is universal, basically human, and exquisitely beautiful.

I will try in many ways here to say that Christmas is a natural rite connected with the passing of seasons and having certain emotional and spiritual qualities. It also has deep roots in the story of Jesus, which is not the same as political and historical Christianity. It's a story of human evolution and utopian vision. Think of Jesus not as the founder of a religion but as a visionary who understands that the transcendent and eternal play an essential role in our humanity.

You don't have to be naive and literal about this transcendence. Keep it intelligent and up to date. But don't get rid of it. One essential ingredient in our humanity is to have an opening to the unknown and the mysterious. Some people refer to this as God, but you don't have to. Skip the language of God if it makes you uncomfortable, but don't give up on Christmas. It will make you a better person and will complete your humanism.

If you are religious and in particular Christian, embrace Christmas but understand it far more deeply than you have to this point. Look at the poetry of it all, and don't be afraid that seeing metaphors and images takes anything away from your devotion and belief. They only deepen your faith.

I am not a secularist, but neither am I an old-time religious believer. I have gone through the transformative passages of depth psychology and world religions in a serious way. I feel that I am more Catholic than ever, more a follower of Jesus than ever in my life. Yet I am as far from a fundamentalist as can be imagined. I don't know anyone who has my particular way of being religious, and that is as it should be. We can each have our own path toward the ultimate depth and vision.

It is in this spirit that I write about Christmas with a passionate desire to make it appealing to the modern man and woman. This festival will give immense benefit to your soul, not in its neurotic forms but in its deep essence. I hope this book allows a route to that essence and inspires people to be both religious and deeply secular, to be in touch with the eternal mysteries and finished with easy religious superficialities.

You can be a modern eclectic seeker, spiritual but not religious, thoughtful, intelligent, and honest, and still enter wholeheartedly into the Christmas mysteries. You can also be an educated and committed Christian and find a path much deeper into the Christmas reality than you have ever known. Just use your intelligence and imagination. Look so deeply into the mysteries of Christmas that you find new life and meaning in the old stories and images. Look closely at the infant in the manger and see your soul making its appearance, full of hope and promise.

CHAPTER ONE

Deepening the Meaning of Christmas

his is a book about Christmas for devout Christians and devout non-Christians—people of other faiths and people of no particular religious attachment, including agnostics and atheists. Christ is in the name of Christmas and so Jesus is central to the festival. But Christ is not contained in Christianity. If you were to read the Gospels in their original Greek, free of the biases of the past, you would behold a man, Jesus, who loves people and life and whose primary activities are to teach and heal. He presents a vision of a world rooted in love, community, and friendship, and these are the themes of Christmas.

I see no evidence that Jesus intended to create a formal religion. That came later. And it has been a very human institution, with much incredible beauty and wisdom and many scandalous follies. I love the Christian tradition, but my mission in life, one of them anyway, is to make the Gospel teaching attractive and accessible to those who are not Christian, and to deepen it for those who are. Christians need more insight, and non-Christians may be surprised to discover the universality in Jesus's message, its intelligence, and its relevance to life today.

In this book I write as one devoted to the story and teachings of Jesus and devoted to speaking to those who are not among his followers. I think Christmas is for everybody. It pains me to hear of disputes about placing nativity scenes in public places. I'd like to see many religious traditions represented in a world where religious freedom means more religion, not less. I rejoice to see a Jewish school or a Muslim mosque or a Buddhist zendo appear in my neighborhood. I hope others will be happy to see a nativity scene at Christmas time.

I write as a theologian, which I define as a professional who investigates the mysteries of life and nature. Some theologians speak from within a religious tradition, but I'm a new kind of theologian who looks at all of life and writes about the mysteries and stories and images that convey them without any institutional connection. While a philosopher might explore ideas and concepts, a theologian focuses on images, narratives, and rituals that express profound truths.

Jesus spoke of a "kingdom of the sky," a life lived by a transcendent and sublime vision and based on love rather than fear and belligerence. In my own translation of the Gospels (published by Skylight Paths), I use the word *sky* rather than *heaven*, since the Greek can mean either. I don't mean that God is literally up among the clouds, but that the sky symbolizes a level of reality different from our everyday practical world. There is one part of us that is engaged in the material life and another part that reaches up toward ideas and values and mysteries that extended the range of our very being. We are both soul and spirit.

Spirit is that urge in us to transcend, to go beyond the person we are and to find as yet undiscovered worlds and sources of meaning. In the spirit we move toward a better future, creative, adventurous, and hopeful. We imagine a community of the world and even of other civilizations on other planets. This spirit we see symbolized in steeples and tall buildings and rockets blasting off. We go to mountains, as Jesus, Moses, and even Socrates did, to be open to inspiration and have grand ideas. Spirit is essential in keeping us alive and in movement.

The soul is quite different. It is found in our mysterious night dreams, in deep memories, and emotions. While the spirit needs detachment from local life so as to be free to explore, the soul prefers being attached to home, close friends and family members, memories and precious objects, places important to us, and even to certain ideas. We think of the soul as operating from the heart. The spirit opens us to possibility, while the soul makes us human and connected to others.

I sometimes speak of this kingdom, this new and visionary way of life, as utopia. I have my namesake, Thomas More, the author of *Utopia*, in the back of my mind. I don't mean an unrealistically positive and perfect form of life, but an evolutionary step beyond where we are. It's my conviction that Jesus was trying to inaugurate this new system of love and community to replace the faulty system of authoritarianism, moralism, dogmatism, and several other "isms." I see Christmas as an experiment in utopian living, lived out each year. The Christmas spirit is the spirit of a new and different way of life.

So I differ from those searching for the true meaning of Christmas as a heavily theological and moral doctrine. I think the popular customs we have in place perfectly express this spirit. Christmas is a sublime festival, but we have forgotten its in-depth meaning and importance.

When you decorate your tree, select your gifts, and have friends over for a party, you are deep into the Christmas spirit and at the heart of its meaning. As we'll see, this Christmas spirit—epitomized in Santa Claus and the Christmas crèche—is the real meaning of Christmas.

CHAPTER TWO

The Day the Sun Stands Still

any people enjoy autumn with its cool nights and shortening days. They are happy to behold the beauty of the colorful leaves and the end of the hot days of summer. For me it's a melancholy time, probably because when I was in my early teens I left home in September for a religious boarding school that wasn't nearly as emotionally warm and comforting as my family. I was homesick in those autumn days, and that pain returns every year when I smell the dying leaves and watch them fall off the trees. Then, as the days grow even shorter, my mood grows darker. I look forward to the winter solstice and the slow return of the sun. Like me, many people find the darkness of late autumn heavy and difficult. People say they get sick and hear of more deaths around this time of year.

Dark days can mean dark moods. This natural turn of the seasons helps explain the timing of Christmas. It is the festival of light, the return of the sun and longer periods of daylight. It's a time of renewal and hope, sentiments we feel as we watch the skies and see faint signs of the sun returning. What happens in December in the northern hemisphere is a natural symbol. You don't need a dictionary or an encyclopedia to know that the dark sky parallels your darkened heart. You feel it in your body and then in your emotions. The sky mirrors your feelings, and your pulse beats with the special rhythms of night and day. The turn of the sun on the day of solstice may well coincide with a turn in your spirits.

This dance of nature and human emotion goes back millennia, for people have always been profoundly affected by the dramatic shift from darkness to light. Christmas did not begin with Jesus. Its deepest mysteries go back to the very beginnings. The Lascaux Caves, oriented toward the summer solstice, go back seventeen thousand years. Stonehenge in England, aligned with the winter solstice sunset, is about three thousand years old.

One of my favorite sacred sites is Newgrange in Ireland, a burial mound and temple constructed 4,500 years ago of huge stones covered with earth. Today you can visit this ceremonial site and crawl through the entranceway, the massive smooth stones rubbing against your body, until you finally stand straight in the central sanctuary. What is especially remarkable about Newgrange is that every year on the winter solstice when the sky is clear, sunlight passes through into the inner sacred space, giving it the only light it has in the year.

If you were to visit Newgrange during the winter solstice, you would enjoy a dramatic display of the origins of Christmas. You would stand in absolute darkness and then be astonished as the sunlight found its way through the carefully designed channel above the entranceway into the inner chamber. The sunlight can penetrate into the chamber only during these special days.

On my last visit to Newgrange, on a typically cool and rainy day, I crouched down almost to my knees to crawl through the low, narrow entrance passage. This is one place in the world where you might imagine the doorway as a birth canal and physically sense a recreation of your coming into the world. That's what I felt on this visit, but it was unusually powerful. I'm seventy-five now, and I think these stark natural rituals speak to me with a new potency. I feel similarly about Christmas. The emotions are now almost as strong as when I was a child.

I'm not saying that the solstice so dramatically experienced at Newgrange is the same as Christmas, but it lies at the origins of the impulse to honor the return of light—the main natural metaphor behind the Christmas celebration. You can't fully appreciate the deep meaning of Christmas unless you reflect on the return of light in both senses: as a natural occurrence well worth celebrating; and as a metaphor for the human experience of going through an emotional dark night only to recover the light of hope and happiness.

Christmas makes sense only if you know the experience of darkness—the experience of not knowing what is going on, not knowing your way, not seeing life for what it is, failing, losing, and suffering. Then the turn toward light has a real impact. The more you know the dark, the more you will appreciate the light.

I feel this solstice archetype when I'm doing therapy with a client who is trying to make sense of a divorce or a sickness or the loss of someone precious. These are dark times, and you can't possibly rush to a solution. You know that there is a natural timing, like the slow days leading up to Christmas, that rules the progress toward light. Knowing the natural rhythm of the solstice helps me be patient and hopeful in these difficult moments.

The word *solstice* means "the sun stands still." *Sol* is the Latin word for sun; *stice* means to stand. Sol-stice is the time when the sun is poised between increase and decrease, a liminal moment outside the ordinary, a time when magic and religion can happen, a time between, not ordinary time but a special time.

The Christmas Veil Is Thin

Christmas is a special time outside of normal time when the veil is thin and the extraordinary breaks into the ordinary, the spiritual into the mundane, and the miraculous into the factual. You hear reindeer on the roof, and a large body falls down through your chimney. You leave cookies and milk out in the evening, and they're gone in the morning. You wake up, and gifts have miraculously appeared around the tree.

Christmas is named after Jesus the Christos, the anointed man. His teaching is a light and a beacon showing the way toward a different way of living, one that is based on mutual respect and courage. His life and his idealistic philosophy are liminal as well— exceptions to the usual ignorance and fear that motivate us.

If you don't have special times in your life that are liminal, that put the ordinary into eclipse, then you are condemned to a dull life of facts and predictability. You have no enchantment, and without the charm of the liminal your soul goes to sleep and you become like a robot. Your very humanity depends on the interplay of the ordinary and the wondrous.

We all know that children are especially susceptible to the thin veil of Christmas, but in our own way we adults could be more open to its impact. You don't have to "believe" in Santa Claus to get into the spirit of the season or to be uplifted by its special charm, but you have to be aware of your need for light and have some hope and vision that light will be there.

THE INTELLIGENCE IN FANTASY

Some people find the Christmas emphasis on fantasy, charm, magic, and sentimentality annoying. These people probably prefer facts and a no-nonsense approach to life. But many of us treasure this special time when the heart comes out of the shadows and rules the day. My own memories of childhood Christmases include attending the Christmas Eve Mass: people coming into the church from the cold, lights everywhere, familiar music going on and on, the warm story of Jesus's birth; and then at home people wishing each other Merry Christmas, smiling and unusually happy. The gifts and sweet and savory foods create a rare atmosphere of carnival and good cheer that transforms life, at least for a day. It's like entering a special room or field where the usual rules of seriousness and heavy matters of consequence give way to simple joy.

Some people don't like those moments when the sun stops in its orbit, midway between winter and summer, and a celebration erupts. They want a more serious festival. A few years ago I was on a radio program broadcast from Dublin, Ireland, shortly before Christmas. I was championing the spirit of Santa Claus, while a popular theologian on the panel was trying to bring people back to heavy teachings about incarnation and divinity. These are beautiful teachings, but I felt the theologian's approach to Christmas was too weighty. He was asking people to be academic and philosophical about the season. He also countered my call for giving Santa Claus a fresh appraisal as the embodiment of joy, saying, as many people do, that we need to put more seriousness back into Christmas. I didn't know why he was in a Bah humbug mood— maybe in reaction to me. Perhaps he caught a whiff of paganism in my position.

We love fantasy in movies and novels, but outside the theater, in life, we want to live in a realm of facts. We suffer a split in our collective psyche with far-reaching fantasy on one side and heavy scientific thinking on the other. Christmas is different in that it is full of fantasy but also serious.

Most children would probably tell you that in their early years Santa Claus was a serious matter, and the day they learned or began to suspect that he wasn't an actual being was a painful bridge out of childhood. As a parent, I was surprised by how strongly I felt the passage in my young daughter's life from belief in Santa to the realization that he is not real in the usual way. One day was especially disturbing, when the man who had played Santa in a school pageant just happened to come into a restaurant where our family was having breakfast. My daughter was quite confused.

I am aware that some psychologists think that an experience like my daughter's is seriously disturbing and therefore we shouldn't foster belief in Santa among children. Yet many of us have gone through the passage to adulthood, losing our so-called belief in Santa, without damage. Maybe it's worse to have the imagination starved or killed off.

I remember my own moment of transition. My mother must have been around thirty. She was standing at the sink washing dishes, and I asked her if Santa was real. "No," she said without any nervousness, "your mother and father are Santa Claus."

I felt some emotional churning, but I had been sifting through the facts and already knew the answer. I just needed confirmation. I agree with the psychologists who explain that this is an important moment in one's orientation toward the world, and I think I made the passage gracefully.

Now I think that my mother wasn't entirely correct. My parents may have given me gifts, but they were not Santa. My parents giving me gifts and telling me stories embodied the spirit of Santa—and they did it very well—but they were not Santa himself. In the realm of imagination, he was as real as the fictional detective Sherlock Holmes, and putting out cookies for him was like adults visiting Sherlock's Baker Street home. Adults can live in an "as-if" world, a place where fiction counts for real.

Expanding your idea of what is true and important is yet another way to get into the spirit of solstice. The sun stands still. The star pauses over the manger. Suddenly and for a brief time, ordinary life fades into the background. We have a chance to reflect on a profound mystery:

The birth of a new kind of person in our society and in ourselves.

Living by facts has its own kind of darkness, and one significant gift of Christmas is to be relieved, at least for a while, of facts. We are an information-based society, but happier societies gave far more serious attention to the old stories that offered guidance as well as entertainment. We have separated wisdom from storytelling, but the Christmas story brings them back together. Part of its light spirit is the relief we feel from living in a disenchanted world, a world made dark and heavy by its devotion to facts.

I used to be quite naive about such things. If you asked me, even in my teens, if the stories of religion are factual, I would have said "Of course." But then I became exposed to scholarship on the Gospel texts and to depth psychology and to literary studies. I developed a more sophisticated and appreciative understanding of symbol, metaphor, and image.

This transformation in understanding has continued all my life, deepening and expanding. One of my great moments in reading came the day I found Norman O. Brown's incomparable book *Love's Body*. Here's a passage that made my pulse jump: "Language is always an old testament, to be made new; rules, to be broken; dead metaphor, to be made alive; literal meaning, to be made symbolical; oldness of letter to be made new by the spirit."[1]

This is a description of Jesus, that infant in the manger. He represents a new law, a new rule of life, for people

THE DAY THE SUN STANDS STILL

who can hear his message. Everything is now different, because of that child. We are transfigured, not the same.

Brown goes on referring to the mysterious moment when Jesus is standing with Moses and Elijah in a vision beheld by his disciples. Brown says, "It is a gathering up of time into eternity; a transfiguration of time; the transfiguration, in which Moses and Elijah, who are the past, appeared unto them as present, talking with Jesus. Symbolical consciousness makes figural interpretations in order to accomplish the transfiguration."[2]

I remember that early theologians, like the great Origen, said that every holy text has its body, soul, and spirit. It is to be read at many levels. It isn't enough to have a child's literal and factual understanding of sacred stories. Christmas is not history; it's mystery.

It took me many years to arrive at this appreciation for the depth of sacred stories. Depth psychology helped me understand that they speak to my inner life. You don't psychologize a holy text like the story of Christmas, but you understand that part of its power comes from how it speaks to your own depths and to the mysterious things that happen to you throughout life.

So solstice is not just a pause, a stopping of the sun; it is also a period of transformation. You can enter this special winter solstice with the aim of being deepened as a person, having your spirituality once again taken further toward insight and wisdom, and appreciating that meta-phor is not a lightening of meaning in a story but a way of allowing meaning to penetrate into your depths.

Solstice is a time of incubation, change and finally of renewal or rebirth. Christmas is a transformation of the soul, but to get to that point you have to appreciate the story of Christmas at a deep level. You have to appreciate the importance and power of metaphor and levels of meaning. You have to tell the story of Jesus's birth again and again until you finally see that it is as much about you as it is about any community of followers. It's all about the mystery by which you become a real person rather than part of the crowd. A real child is born within you.

THE STILLPOINT OF THE REVOLVING SUN

Christmas is like a hole in the calendar, or at least a blank space. At Christmas time we take a break from the ordinary and turn some of our serious rules upside down. At this time we may spend more money than usual, if we have it, eat foods off our normal diet, and invite people we rarely see to our homes. These momentary indulgences are of absolute importance because they speak to the soul. They take our attention away from duties and money-making to being with friends and family.

In some countries Christmas had a "Lord of Misrule," someone to lead people as they overturned many of the rules of ordinary polite society. Older cultures could be even more radical in allowing otherwise forbidden practices during the liminal time of solstice.

A festival is usually joyous and may involve games and other forms of good cheer. In America on the Fourth of July you're likely to hear loud bangs from firecrackers and see bright and colorful fireworks bursting in the sky. Those same songs and sights may not be tolerated so well outside the time of festival, when we're back in ordinary time. It's typical for the special liminality of festival to allow behavior that is usually not permitted, and so it is often a time of liberation and discovery.

The excesses common during the Christmas season—too many gifts, too much partying, traveling great distances to see family members—are part of this traditional license common to festivals, especially, as we'll see, those festivals associated with the solstices. It's tempting to judge ourselves and others for going too far, but it might be more in the spirit of the season to find it in ourselves to allow such excesses. The whole idea is to drop some of the limitations that we usually bring to serious areas of life and be free momentarily of their weight.

As a child on Christmas day I had the strong sensation that time had stopped. We spent the whole day doing nothing but eating and opening gifts. My uncles spread out on couches and soft chairs and snored for hours. I never saw them do that on any other day. The sun stops, and for a moment you don't know if it's going to go forward or backward. In sympathy, life stops, too. My uncles stopped rather noisily.

The solstice—the sun stopping in its tracks—is akin to Alice going down the rabbit hole or through the looking glass. In the special realm below or behind the ordinary, many things are backwards. In solstice time, what is usually considered unacceptable is allowed. You may sleep late, visit many people, and eat unhealthy food. You can buy things for yourself and others without any guilt.

This same rule applies to the Christian celebration of the birth of Jesus. He was a child of the solstice. (Of course, the Church chose the date of December 25 to make a theological point; it is a date that is spiritually imaginal and meaningful.) His teachings recommend making all of life liminal, suspending the usual ways of doing things and becoming less judgmental and more loving. In other words, his way is a break from things as usual. When you follow his way, your whole life is a hiatus and an exception to the way the world works. He taught that the old moralism and dogmatism were outdated and inhumane. In their place he suggested the law of love.

In the Christmas story we read about the birth of Jesus and picture the infant lying in a feeding trough, a star stopped in its movement over the scene of the birth. The stars stops. Time pauses. Liminality begins. In a sense we are in an unusual time when we stop the ways of the world and give utopia a chance.

This was my experience of Christmas as a child, as well. Time stopped. People behaved beautifully but oddly. Why were they so happy and why use the word *merry* on this one day of the year? You never say "Merry Monday" or "Merry Easter." "Merry" belongs to Christmas and sets it apart.

If you decide to follow the Jesus way—for example, his teachings on radical love and care for those outside your circle—and become a full-time healer, instinctively adopting a healing posture whenever you see trouble or suffering, then you know what Christmas is all about. It's the birth of this sensibility in you. Maybe you've been taught, "Don't spoil your children." At Christmas time you can break that rule.

Here's an important law of life you probably didn't learn at school: It's as important to break rules as it is to keep them. Jesus was a great rule-breaker. The religious leaders told Jesus not to heal on the Sabbath, because you weren't supposed to do anything on that day. He went ahead and did his healing and teaching anyway, because he was there to mark the end of religious legalism. If people were suffering on the Sabbath, he would heal them.

I left monastic life in my mid-twenties and have gone on to create a way of life that on the outside looks more secular. But deep down I still feel like a monk. When I chose to be a psychotherapist, I was fully aware that to follow the Jesus way means to be a healer in a serious way. I still practice therapy, and I still see it as following through on the Jesus model of being a healer at all times, whenever the occasion demands it.

For me, Christmas is the prime opportunity to renew the birth of that child with his new vision for humanity in myself. The vision is born in me once again, for the seventieth time at least, and I'm ready to live a life that is a challenge to the way of the world with its self-interest, excessive aggression and failure to heal.

People usually think of Christmas as a traditional and sentimental festival, but not as a celebration of the Jesus vision it commemorates: a philosophy of profound reform. The child lying in the manger would become perhaps the most radical of all spiritual visionaries, showing how to live more joyfully and communally.

Many people today feel an underlying anxiety due to world events and the challenges of getting along in a complicated world. Christmas allows a break from that gray depression, an inner darkness reflected in the late autumn sky. Solstice offers symbolic hope that there may be a turn in the "weather." The turn could take us to more genuine peace, justice, and community—key values in the Jesus teachings and qualities we expect in a renewed life turning more toward the light than the dark.

CHAPTER THREE

The Birth of the Child

ne day I had the opportunity to sit down for a conversation with a well-known columnist and television personality. I had hoped to discuss our mutual experience of speaking to the public and sticking our necks out. Instead, he asked me if my name is a stage name. He thought I might have taken it because of its history. People often remark on my name, thinking of the connection with the Irish poet Thomas Moore or the English saint and statesman Thomas More.

I assured my famous friend that my father was Thomas Moore, as was his father, and I haven't gone back to research further. But the question got me thinking about names and how I have felt an affinity with Thomas More of England, who was interested in many of the things that shape me: humanism, scholarship, the arts, music, architecture, the Italian Renaissance, theology, and education. The name at birth can be very significant.

Christmas takes its name from Jesus Christ—Christ Mass. Christ, *Christos* in Greek, means anointed and, when taken back far enough, olive oil. I like to call Jesus "The Man of Olive Oil," an image as rich in meaning as it is simple. It is fairly well known that Christ is like chrism, an oil used to anoint a spiritual leader. Jesus is the Messiah, the anointed man. But the metaphor goes much further and touches on the most radical aspect of Jesus's message.

You've probably never thought of the olive oil on your dinner table as one of the most awesome of symbols. When you make a salad for a special dinner, you don't just serve plain lettuce and tomatoes. You "dress" the salad with oil. Oil takes the experience to a different level of taste. You go from utterly plain, maybe even dull, to interesting and flavorful. The oil shifts your experience from eating plants to enjoying a salad. It raises up an ordinary meal a considerable notch.

Here, in such a simple thing as oil, we have the perfect clue to the whole point of Jesus's teaching. He wanted us to raise up our lives a considerable notch: from unconscious, moralistic self-interest to a highly civilized and spiritually sophisticated life based on love and community. Unconscious living is like lettuce without oil, plants instead of salad, cold nutrition instead of warm dining. Jesus brings the oil of a soulful and spiritually elevated awareness to ordinary life, which otherwise tends to be full of unnecessary prejudice and aggression.

Jesus uses other similar homespun images for this shift in the quality of life. They are usually embedded in parables —salt, yeast, wine, water, a mustard seed—something small planted in you that becomes the very spark of life. Maybe the most powerful of these metaphors appears in the story of the Wedding Party at Cana, where Jesus changes the water of purification into wine for a party. The difference between plain water and wine is, metaphorically speaking, the difference between an unconscious, loveless, and unremarkable way of life versus an intensely communal, open-minded, loving, fearless, and dedicated life.

It's easy to pass over this key technique that Jesus uses: He takes the simplest of kitchen and dinner items and uses them as the basic metaphors for his proposal for a new way of life. It may take a lifetime to go through the change of heart and vision needed to become a truly evolved person, but if you succeed you will have added yeast to your life and transformed the water of your plain existence into the wine of a deeply satisfying way of being.

Maybe you can see how closely this Jesus teaching and the spirit of Christmas go together? Christmas focuses on family, giving, general good cheer, and the renewal of life. The infant in the manger embodies nothing less than a new kind of human being. He is yet another image for the great transformation. He is the new human, elevated, evolved, and brought to a new level of perfection. No wonder angels appeared to celebrate the event!

Language about a divine child and a new humanity may get you to thinking that no one, certainly not you, can actually reach that level. We are all plain lettuce, lumps of flour without yeast. But I have met many men and women in my life that I consider truly evolved, not perfect, but very human, and yet they had a persistent excellence and goodness of heart that, to me, proves they were anointed.

One remarkable and perhaps unlikely example from my life may illustrate what I'm saying. In my second year of high school at a Catholic seminary, we were introduced to a new English teacher, Father Gregory O'Brien.

He was a very worldly man in that he loved gourmet food, good restaurants, and parties and nights on the town. Part of his worldliness was his love of the arts—painting, dance, architecture, music, theater. But he was also devout at prayer and reverent at our Masses and liturgies. We students generally loved him and felt his love for us. We knew that he would do anything for us, and we admired his highly cultured blend of spirituality and worldliness.

His progressive ideas made him the object of mockery among some members of his community, but the constant criticism didn't wear him down or cause him to lose his buoyant sense of humor. He suffered rejection and disapproval—the Jesus archetype of visionary teacher persecuted by those who don't want to wake up—but he pressed on in a utopian spirit.

Sixty years later, I still think of Father O'Brien and feel grateful for the example he gave me. I still try to emulate him by blending the best of worldliness with a reverent but progressive form of spirituality. He was a special being, certainly at a level above most.

At our own birth, the child of Christmas is born in us. He is our spiritual potential. But we have to let that birth find its fulfillment in a life that rises above the ordinary. You might say that we have to keep the promise of that child alive in us always. Christmas is a reminder that the child is always being born, always in the manger, and always being welcomed.

What happened on Christmas day was no ordinary birth. The baby is surrounded by animals, angels, and foreign "wise men." If you take the story of Christmas only as history and fact, you may not be able to make it your own. See through these images to their deeper meaning. Wise men from afar come to honor the child, and if you become a person of great vision a wider world will be yours. Angels sing in joy, just as your birth to a higher level will be something for the world to applaud. If you don't reach a new level of existence, rooted in ideals and a compassionate way of life, Christmas won't really happen. It will remain a mere possibility.

THE BIRTH OF THE KINGDOM

A parable not often told in churches comes from the Gospel of Thomas, perhaps the most important of the non-official, noncanonical Gospels. Some of these Gospels are quite different from the New Testament Gospels, but the Gospel of Thomas for the most part tells the usual teachings without much narrative. These Gospels in general give a broad picture of Jesus's personality and purpose, as they also add color to our view of what Jesus wanted to accomplish. In this story, Jesus compares the kingdom to a woman who buys a sack of seeds in her village and then walks home. As she walks the seeds all gradually fall out through a hole in the sack. So when the woman gets home, the sack is empty. This is the kingdom!

This story would be familiar to anyone who has read Eastern spiritual literature, where emptiness is a beloved teaching. Perhaps the most honored of all Buddhist chants, the Heart Sutra, teaches that everything in life and personality is empty. Empty not in a nihilistic or depressive way, but in the sense that nothing we cling to is the final answer, and everything has infinite layers of significance. We can't define or limit the mystery of our existence. When the devout Buddhist teacher says, "if you see the Buddha on the road, kill him," he is warning against making Buddhism or the Buddha too weighty or literal. You must see through even your most precious ideas and beliefs.

The Jesus kingdom can't survive if it is taken too literally or desperately. Christmas, too, needs a little emptiness. I remember once bringing my children to a church service at Christmas where the kind pastor had a little rite in which the children could place large, heavy figures into the nativity scene. Of course, there were many more children than characters in the Christmas story, so there was a steady behind-the-scenes activity bringing the figures back and forth from the crèche to the children. It was a practical solution, but I thought it also nicely deconstructed the scene, as the figures came and went, now there and now gone. The ending of the Heart Sutra is sometimes translated as "Gone, gone, completely gone."

If you think you understand everything there is to know about Christmas, then your understanding isn't empty in this spiritual sense. To be too certain of anything is to lack the virtue of emptiness. If you think you own your views and others don't, then you are not sufficiently empty. Christmas is a mystery, not a fact. If you can keep the mystery alive, it will remain a living ritual feeding you every year.

The kingdom is empty also in that it turns logic upside down. It empties out what we think is right and true. Jesus tells the story of a foreman hiring several people at different times of the day to work in a vineyard. At the end of the day they all get paid the same. There's no logic in this story, but in the kingdom this is how things work. You have a community in which everyone, first to last, has equal value.

The general idea is that to follow the Jesus vision you have to let go of the logic of the ordinary world. That may be one of the great stumbling blocks, for many people try hard to be both standard members of society and followers of Jesus. They don't understand the radical nature of Jesus's teaching about love and community. To be in the kingdom you may have to be slightly insane to the rest of the world, and this faithful insanity is yet another kind of emptiness.

THE IMAGE OF THE CHILD

In the same spirit Jesus points out that the kingdom is really for children. They aren't fully adjusted to the rules of society and so, like mad people, they, too, live by a different logic. A child might well pay the same amount to people who work longer or shorter hours.

You could think of Christmas in this way, as a festival for children who live more by a gift economy than by a structure based on work. At Christmas we could all restore some of the enchanted, open, unspoiled other-worldliness of the child.

Christmas is the time to focus on the child: your child-hood, perhaps your children, the world's children, your child spirit, fragile beginnings, innocent rejection of the world's adult ways. It the season to be unreasonably generous, interested in toys, and given to playing games and giving attention to dolls and puppets and electric trains.

The positive, affirming and hopeful teaching of Jesus is not only foreseen in the infant of the nativity, it is also symbolized by that child. When any child is born, we have no idea what he or she will become. The possibilities are infinite, and therefore the child represents a new being. He is not a copy; he is an original.

Christmas, whether it commemorates the birth of the infant at Bethlehem or the return of sunshine, is about the hope for new and abundant life. Christmas is a celebration for the soul, because the soul is the principle of life and vitality. The Greek word for soul, *psyche,* means "breath"; and the Latin *anima* leads to our English word *animate*, which means "come to life" or be "full of life". The child reminds us of the infinite possibilities of life available to us, and we celebrate that vitality in the season of good cheer, gift-giving and community.

When I was a child I felt the magic of Christmas in my very being. If there is such a thing as a resurrected body, that is who I was on Christmas Day. My whole family together evoked that magic and laid an important foundation for me as a religious person and someone open to enchantment. I didn't know at that time that seventy years later I'd be writing about Christmas having a depth of meaning I have never read about elsewhere. My early experience of Christmas is now fulfilled in a way I would never have anticipated, and now I feel that this book comes out of my enchantment with the solstice, the Jesus philosophy, and my parents' good will.

By the way, when I mention "the Jesus philosophy," I want to emphasize the role of Jesus in giving us a worldview that differs from the one we live by today. For him, human interactions are based on the model of friendship; love is the main dynamic, but it is not so personal or sentimental, and rather than go around being productive he teaches and models an approach based on healing. This is a different way of being in the world, a new philosophy.

But my sense of Christmas is also different now. I understand better that Jesus was addressing all people on the planet, not wanting them to join his organization but to adopt his vision for a better human race. I now see how Christmas and Jesus's vision line up, and I see that the enchantment of Christmas is a taste of what would be possible if human beings could really love each other. Given all of that, I understand how the infant in the manger symbolizes the new life in me, the potential I have to be a new kind of being dedicated to *agape*, to a love of the other whoever he or she is.

This is a remarkable mystery worthy of celebration and suitable in any setting on earth. It makes no sense to see it exclusively as a ritual for Christians. It has meaning only as a plan for the entire human race—and therefore Christmas belongs to everyone.

It's easy to be profoundly cynical about the possibility of a world living by love. So many find the idea of utopia and of Jesus's proposal about loving your enemies not just preposterous but naive and fantastical. It will never happen, they think, and if you expect it, you are not acquainted with the ways of the world. To these people, utopia is a wonderful, wishful fantasy, and an unrealistic, childish illusion.

A somewhat easier approach to utopia is to see it as a way of imagining an ideal future, and you strive toward it knowing that you will never fully achieve it. This kind of utopia keeps you on track. You hope for a perfect life, and that hope allows you to steadily improve. Your ideal motivates you.

But I don't get the impression that this is the kind of world Jesus was recommending. In an important set of words, he frequently said that the "kingdom of the sky" or "the kingdom of God" is drawing near. Then he made two key points about this situation: 1) Be prepared. Don't be left out in the cold. There will be two kinds of people: those in this utopia and those outside it. You don't want to be in the old arrangement. 2) Don't presume that you will be part of the new regime simply because you are Jewish or Christian or virtuous, believing that of course you will be "in." Just the opposite: Many people who for external reasons think they're automatically part of it will be left out.

You have to *live* this new way to be a member of the new community. You have to get the point that it's all about a reversal of values. Financial success in this utopia could be an obstacle, not a measure of success. So give up that idea. That's why the small-scale, experimental gift-economy of Christmas is so important. It's a tiny example of a new way of life, a one-day utopia, when we don't demand a quid-pro-quo financial economy. Generosity is the thing, not financial shrewdness.

As a psychotherapist practicing a kind of depth psychology, I'm well acquainted with the shadow side of life and how imperfect the lives of well-intentioned people can be. I'm aware of my own failures and short-comings. The same parents who gave me such wonderful Christmases also passed on emotional habits that have made my own life difficult, and some of those generational problems were due to religion. But I still believe in utopia, the kingdom of the sky, and I still think that Christmas is worth celebrating wholeheartedly.

As a therapist I've witnessed people dealing with significant failings in their childhood yet growing up to become beautiful, if not perfect, adults. They may not know themselves well, and they may struggle with certain issues in their lives, but through these very limitations they find beautiful solutions.

I don't look for perfection, but for joy and happiness. At Christmas we don't wish each other perfect lives but only "comfort and joy." This is what I look for: not an end to struggle, but a level of understanding and adjustment so that we can say to each other, "Merry Christmas."

In a similar way, it isn't necessary to be physically healthy to appreciate the joy of Christmas. In our society currently we make a big thing of health, so much so that we seem to be constantly thinking about how to be healthier. In many instances our preoccupation with health, though obviously good to a degree, seems excessive and full of anxiety. Paradoxically, we worry ourselves to death trying to be healthy.

The Christmas ideal is different. Yes, take care of your health. But understand how important it is and how central to the Christmas message, to be merry, to have a hopeful, positive, and optimistic attitude, even if your health is bad or if life is not at its best. The infant Jesus is lying in a barnyard crib, and yet the emotional atmosphere is glorious and full of hope. What a lesson for us living in a time of worldwide conflict and personal challenges.

I don't have a hygienic approach to life, and I don't wish you a healthy Christmas. People can be unhealthy physically and emotionally and yet still be merry. In the kingdom I imagine, people find their beauty as much in their shortcomings and failures as in their strengths and successes. Utopia arrives when people stop pretending to be perfect or aiming in that direction and finally confront their dark sides. After depth psychology, we have to reimagine what it means to create a beautiful world. We don't aim for perfection but for what the Japanese call *wabi-sabi*—the beauty of the imperfect and the fading. I wish you a *wabi-sabi* Christmas.

Notice how often I speak of beauty. Because we have been so deeply influenced by moralistic philosophies in our history, especially a misguided interpretation of the Jesus message as moralistic, we think of our goal as perfection—a blameless life. Instead, we could see the beautiful as our most excellent future. For myself, I can say that I hope that my life and that of my family is beautiful. I don't expect perfection or unblemished health.

So, go on saying "Merry Christmas." Don't say, "To your health," as important as health may be. This festival transcends health. Even if your health is bad, you can be merry. Don't say, "I wish you a year without sin."

Christmas transcends moral anxiety. You can easily detect anxiety in people who worry about sinful action on the part of others instead of their own sinful action. That is not being merry, and it's against the Christmas spirit.

Yes, be ethical. But your ethics can be rooted in your utopian vision of a world based on love and community. That is Jesus morality, radically different because good behavior is motivated by love. I say, "Jesus morality," because Gospel ethics are different from the dos and don'ts we often associate with living a moral life. You don't get stern warnings or lists of bad behavior from Jesus. Instead, you find a way of being moral that is positive and supportive. You're good because you love and respect people and have worked through your self-interest and other forms of narcissism. You've tamed the passions that make you a danger to others.

The Christmas greeting is not about good behavior but about being merry, seeing the beauty and goodness of life, in spite of all the bad stuff.

Thomas More, the author of *Utopia*, commonly said to his family and friends: "Pray that we will meet merrily in heaven." He especially used this phrase when he was in a cold, vaulted room in the tower of London waiting for his execution. Once I visited that cell and "heard" his words reverberate across the cone-shaped walls. I've always enjoyed his word *merrily* with its slight hint of Christmas, and I hope that I can be as dedicated to a sacred world as my namesake was in prison.

On an ordinary day you may suddenly realize that life is full of gifts, and you may think, "It's like Christmas." Christmas is not just a time of year, not just a festival. It's an archetype of life's generosity and giving. We encounter it all year long and celebrate it at the time of solstice.

Whenever you step away from the unconscious, ego-centered ways of the world and try to live in a different milieu, the kind that Jesus exemplified and spelled out in his teaching, then Jesus is born. Christmas happens; it is not a one-time historical event. At Christmas time we don't memorialize an event from history; rather, we acknowledge and call to mind a deep archetypal event that can take place at any moment. Jesus could be born.

You may suddenly discover that money, though not negative in itself, is not the key to happiness. You learn through some great fortune that friendship and love are infinitely more important. At that moment Jesus is born.

When some new possibility for your life stirs in you, something heretofore unknown and unfamiliar, Jesus is born. It is Christmas. When suddenly you realize that you can open your heart in love, when you have kept it closed for years out of fear, it is Christmas. When you consider how to spend your time, and you go to a hospital to visit the sick, Jesus is born and it is Christmas.

Christmas is an archetypal event, deep within, and outside of history. Christmas is a mystery: It is not a puzzle to be figured out but a mysterious happening that trans-figures life and gives it meaning. It makes life merry and worthy of our complete devotion.

CHAPTER FOUR

The Manger and the Animals

There was no room in the inn. No room for this woman, who much later would be called the Queen of Heaven; for the man Joseph, after whom countless hospitals and churches would be named; for the child whom theologians would call divine and the son of God. The story of Jesus is full of such reversals.

It's difficult to understand the natural conundrum by which good people are rejected and persecuted, but it happens every day. We celebrate Martin Luther King Jr. with a holiday today, but I remember when King was doing his work and many good people—some of them my own friends and family members—were speaking of him with scorn and warning that he was "just stirring up trouble." Good Christians, many of these detractors.

Some think that the "inn" was really a "guest room," perhaps in a family house. Mary and Joseph might not have been rejected but just crowded out with family members and forced to use a room where you might find animals. But the idea of a great figure being born in a lowly place and in need of a temporary home still holds.

Those who study great heroes and divine and semi-divine figures point out that their stories often tell of abandonment in childhood. Baby Moses floats down the river in a basket. Romulus and Remus are left to exposure and raised by a wolf and a woodpecker before they grow up to found the city of Rome. Harry Potter is a child orphan living with adoptive parents outside the magical realm where he belongs before he becomes a hero.

In a larger sense, we are all orphans, looking for a family and parents. We hope to find them in the workplace and in the neighborhood. Usually we find adequate father and mother figures, a family community of sorts, and a good enough home. But the ache and the yearning often remain. There is often no room in the inn.

In my own story, there came a point when I was practicing as a therapist in Texas. I had a license and quite a few clients. I felt I could be successful. But I was from Michigan and found the Texas culture foreign. I liked many aspects of it, but I yearned for a more familiar setting. So one day I set out in my car, stuffed with all the things I felt I needed, and headed for New England. I just felt that there I might more likely find a real home.

My intention was to get a teaching post somewhere and get settled. So I visited many small colleges and institutes, thinking that one of them would like to employ my talents. But one by one they closed their doors and told me to look elsewhere. I finally gave up my search, because obviously for me there was no room in the inn. I had to find a different kind of family and a different source of security.

I felt I had something valuable to offer, but no one seemed to recognize it. People think sentimentally that they would never turn Jesus away. But he himself said,

"Whatever you failed to do for the least of these people, you failed to do for me." I hope I learned from my experience of rejection to be very careful turning people away myself. The Jesus ideal, the very basis of my life, is at stake.

The story of Jesus is not that of a hero. He doesn't overcome his enemy. He favors love over action. "Put down your sword," "the first shall be last," "give away everything you have"—this Taoist-like philosophy is his vision for the world. In many ways, Jesus is an anti-hero.

But Jesus begins as heroes usually do, rejected by the world he has come to serve and heal. There is no room in the inn. There is little room in the world for a true visionary, especially one with the persuasive power, comprehensive scope, and psychological depth that Jesus has.

He understands that an unsentimental but deeply felt sense of neighbor is necessary for a new level of intimate and social interaction. He appreciates that every life has its wounds and is in need of healing. He knows that people are compelled by their various inner forces—we, too, refer to them as our demons—that need clearing out. He even understands the effectiveness of good stories, strong images and potent rituals. At one point he says, "I speak in parables."

Believers consider Jesus to be divine. But to enter into the real spirit of Christmas you don't have to be that kind of believer. You can appreciate the absolute need for Jesus's teachings and celebrate those on this special day, without accepting the entire complex theology. Of course, if you're a believer you're well on your way to appreciating the deep meaning of Christmas.

You reflect on the baby in the manger, a meager setting for the arrival of a world-changing visionary. You grasp the paradox by which the most precious challenge for a better world first appears in the lowliest of settings. Later, Jesus will teach the bittersweet lesson that the last will be first and the first last. You may catch a hint of the essence of the Jesus way, and everything you think you understand about life will be turned upside down.

The manger reminds us, too, that our own spiritual beginnings are humble. We have much to learn about life, and it's likely that we too will live for a while with some anxiety about our worth and with exaggerated concerns about having everything we need. Eventually, if we have the good fortune to arrive at a higher level of under-standing, entering the kingdom in our own way, we will complete our mission. We will evolve into loving, neigh-borly, healing, self-possessed beings, as Jesus did.

Peaceful and Humble

Jesus's life would not be as peaceful and bucolic as his birth. His piercing, positive message stirred up trouble, and many thought that he was a threat to settled reli-gious ideas and structures and even to political stability. At the same time, the traditional sense of quiet and serenity associated with the stables and pastures of the Christmas scene portray a humility that is another hallmark of Jesus in the Gospels.

In modern life, many people pull away from the crowds of shoppers and heavy drinking that appear as Christmas approaches. They may seek some peace and comfort with relatives over good food and conversation. In my family, we have always exchanged gifts Christmas morning, carefully distinguishing between bounty and excess.

The lowly manger could remind us that one of the main themes of Jesus's teaching is genuine humility: the willingness to be vulnerable, not in control, and open to influence. It's a subtle teaching that steers a good course between sadism and masochism, between wanting to dominate people and subjecting yourself too much. There is no room in the inn or no spare room in the house, and so you are humbled; you are required to go out to the stable where animals and shepherds are your company, where comforts are basic and natural.

We could bring some of this humility into our celebration of Christmas by giving gifts that are not excessive in price or quantity, perhaps hand-crafted or carefully hunted down. One Christmas my stepson Abe spent hours just before the holiday sawing, sanding and finishing blocks of walnut wood that he shaped into beautiful boxes. I once stayed up late on Christmas Eve finishing a cherry night table I had made for my wife. There is something deeply personal and full of love in carefully planned, handmade gifts. You can imagine going out to the barn to do the work.

In the lives of all of us, usually there comes a day when the world says "there is no room in the inn." You're fired from a job, or not hired. You don't feel welcome in someone's home, or in your neighborhood. Some project you've worked hard at isn't appreciated. A person you like and want to be with tells you to look elsewhere.

One day, after I had had some success as an author but my fifteen minutes of fame had passed, I received a letter in the mail from the director of a prestigious psychological treatment center that I had always held in high esteem. They had an opening for a director and wondered if I would like come for an interview for the position. Suddenly I was filled with fantasies of creating a soul-centered institute of care and study. I couldn't believe the sheer luck to be considered for the position. This institute happened to be located in one of my favorite areas in the country. An added bonus was that I'd have some financial security after years of trying to make a living as a writer. So I wrote back and said I'd love to come for an interview.

I waited and waited. Finally, a sad letter came back. "This was a clerical error. We're not interested in you. Please don't write back." No room in the inn. I know what that pattern in life is all about. You make more of a possibility about something being offered to you than the people who are offering it. Then it's taken away anyway.

These moments are difficult to take, and you may feel like giving up or fighting back. The nativity scene suggests looking elsewhere, even if the alternative is far less attractive than the place that rejected you. Rejection is humbling, but humiliation can be an invitation to genuine humility. You have to take in the refusal, holding it and reflecting on it. No reacting. No self-pity. The nativity scene is not a tragic event but glorious. "No room in the inn" turned into "Glory to God in the highest." "Joy to the world." "Silent night, holy night."

What emerges from no room at the inn is the life of Jesus, the Gospel itself. You have to open yourself wide enough to have room for rejection. The packed inn, the rustic manger, the breath of animals—all of this is part of the Christmas scene, your birth into who you can be. Rejection turns the ground over so that something can grow.

THE ABANDONED CHILD

They pushed Moses off in a basket and into a river according to the old and familiar story of the abandoned hero. He belongs to the world, not to his personal family, as at a point we all will. There may be a turning point where fate pushes us out and onto a body of water so that we can drift to where we need to be. The hero—the hero in us all—has a larger destiny, and therefore has parents of another order: not biological but spiritual.

Look at a painting of the annunciation and you will see the dove hovering over the virgin. She is conceiving something divine, and a human being eventually is born. This is a spiritual conception, an impregnation of the soul, using metaphors of human biology for a spiritual event. The scene gives image to the appearance of a new being. It also shows what can happen to us as we encounter the spiritual realm and find new life in us.

There is our physical birth and the birth of our soul into the special world of our parents and larger family, and even our culture. But then there is further birth as we enter our destiny and become a person in a larger sense. Our world expands, but as it does we have to be born to another level of being.

Christmas is a celebration of this spiritual birth, of the child in us that is destined to make a real contribution to the world. There is no room in the inn for us, and that forces us to go out into the world among shepherds, ordinary strangers just doing their work. Angels sing in praise, because when a person is born the world hopes that this may be "the one"—a real leader and a true teacher.

Often people have too small a sense of their own destiny and fail to grow into their bigness. They remain in hiding and don't enjoy the rewards of being a player on the world stage. But if, at Christmas, they were to identify with the infant Jesus, they might understand that we ordinary folks are not meant to live only for our own enjoyment. We have a role to play in the unfolding of the world. It isn't enough to remain in the comfortable home of your personal family, attached to your parents and the small world in which you grew up. You have to cross a threshold and find different parents and a new home. If you don't, you remain infantile. But if you do, you learn that there is no end to being born.

All my life I've reflected on the months when I was thirteen, inflamed with a desire to become a priest and planning to leave my warm and loving home for the cool realm of an all-male seminary and monastery. Often I wish I had never left but had stayed home and enjoyed life with my wonderful parents and brother and other kind and happy members of my large extended family. But then I remember that leaving brought me into a much larger world. I studied just what I needed to focus on to become the writer I am. Who knows what would have happened had I stayed home. But the likelihood is that I would have lived in a much smaller world.

Christmas is not the story of an ordinary birth. It tells of a miraculous delivery in which a savior of the world was born. That is the destiny of us all. Christmas puts us in touch with the identity we would have if we responded in all our greatness. No false humility. No holding back. No retreat into the comforts of home when the world is desperate for our contribution. We have to do our part to save the world.

Meditate on the manger and see yourself lying there in the straw. Whoever you are, whatever your beliefs, let this scene goad you on to another level, toward a greater self that belongs to the world. That baby honored by foreign visitors and angels is you, and if you don't realize that, you are missing out on the greatest secret of Christmas.

No one would choose to be born in a barn, or in a feeding trough on top of it. A spirit of poverty and humility are essential. You don't go after your own gain primarily but often have to sacrifice your needs for the greater good. You learn that people won't understand what you are trying to do. Even your most exalted aims may be misunderstood and criticized. You have no choice but to be humble and just go ahead with your life work. It all unfolds exactly as told in the story of Bethlehem, the shepherds, and the manger.

THE WARMING BREATH OF ANIMALS

In the Gospel story of Jesus's birth you don't hear of animals, but tradition puts them there, probably because of the reference to a manger and shepherds. It's said that the animals breathing on the child kept him warm. But I imagine that, like many children, this precocious baby had an understanding with the animals. Today the Christmas crèche would be incomplete without them.

Among other things, the animals remind us of the cosmic destiny of this child, that he will become a spiritual leader with a message that will alter the way people live on the planet. His kingdom implies a different relation to the natural world and to animals, to the universe as a whole, and to all its particulars.

He was called "The Lamb of God" because he was sacrificed for the good of humankind, and at the mention in the story of shepherds, we can easily imagine lambs at his birth. I would be sure to put lambs in my nativity scene. I remember them from childhood—puffs of wool with simple stick legs.

I'd also include cows and a bull, partly because the cows are traditional and the bull brings to mind the astrological sign of Taurus in all its earthiness. Certainly the nativity scene is both heavenly and earthly. The connection may be distant, but we could see the animals surrounding the child as a zodiac, placing the event in a cosmic context, and emphasizing the theme of destiny that is so strong in the story.

Perhaps the most important role of the animals is to show the intimate connection between the Jesus vision and the natural world. He became not just a social reformer but a complete visionary whose teachings affect every aspect of life, including the natural world in which we live. Christmas, with the images of the tree and the animals, marks the renewal of all life.

St. Francis of Assisi referred to animals as our brothers and sisters. We are all earth beings, connected and mutually dependent. Actually, we are not on the planet, but of it. We grow out of the earth like trees and lambs, and it's a great mystery how our souls come into being. The appearance of the human soul, central to what happens in Bethlehem, is a mystery that only makes sense if we imagine the earth itself as a being with a soul. There is much more to the planet than meets the eye or can be measured, and that mystery lies deep within the narrative of Jesus's birth.

The joy we feel in Christmas parties and gift-giving and special dinners and reuniting families points to a different way of living here. We can understand that all who are born of this earth make up a family—not just human-kind but all flora and fauna. If we were really to reunite at Christmas, we would bring along all the animals and plants that live around us. My little cotton-stick lambs and the shiny star on top of the tree teach us this.

Most of the great religions begin with a simple story: Adam and Eve can't resist a piece of fruit and are chased out of Paradise; the Buddha breaks out of his quarantine and beholds suffering and death; Mohammed has a world-changing encounter with an angel in a cave; Moses can't see the Promised Land. There is no place for Jesus in the comfortable moneyed world of hotels and inns, and so he has to come into life among shepherds and amid the sweet and acrid smells of a barn.

But the Jesus story foretells the style of his life and the thread of his teaching. He would tell an outrageous little joke: It's easier for a camel to pass through the eye of a needle than for a wealthy person to enter the kingdom. Many read this story as one about the difficulty of following the Jesus way, but we could also put the accent on the camel. It's easier for an animal, because animals already live in the style of the kingdom. In comparison to us, sometimes they can do the impossible.

THIS KINGDOM AND THAT KINGDOM

The difference between the inn and the manger is similar to the contrast between the realm of the angel and that of Mary in the annunciation. We saw that in art they are separated by a wall or a plant or some gate-like barrier. The realm above and the one below may interact, but they are different, and there is a barrier or veil between them.

The manger lies directly under the night stars and is therefore situated in its cosmic context. What happens there is not domestic but global and even cosmic. In your living room the manger at the bottom of the tree or on your mantel is related to the star at the top of the tree or on your presents. At Christmas we are meant to be under the stars. That may be why some Christians celebrate midnight Mass. The star is essential, as is the manger.

In our day, we miss out on some of the symbolism of Christmas because we look at the world as scientists. We are taught from an early age to see the natural world as a collection of objects that have no meaning in themselves. The sun is an orb in the sky, a star like the many stars we behold at night. But people in the past looked at that sun and saw hope, knowledge, vitality, and personality. What we call "the heavens" was heaven, a spiritual realm full of meaning.

The manger, at least in popular tradition, is out there in the fields at night, under the full display of mysterious darkness and equally mysterious light. Imagine the manger as a simple, homespun planetarium. The birth taking place there has meaning for the whole universe. And that is what Christmas is. It honors what is possible in this world: the birth of a creature who can transform the entire universe by the power of his imagination and his vision for a better world.

If we could evolve to the point of global peace, the possibilities for human creativity would be astounding, and that creativity would have an impact in the universe just as human activity today affects the planet. In the imagery of the great Catholic scientist-theologian Teilhard de Chardin, an increase in our awareness is an essential part of the evolution of humanity and the world in which we live.

Teilhard studied evolving human beings at the scientific level, playing a significant role, for example, in the discovery of "Peking Man." But he was also a Catholic priest, and he understood that physical evolution becomes spiritual evolution. For him, the birth of Christ was a key moment in that evolution. In his book *The Future of Man* he wrote: "Christ is the term *of even the natural* evolution of living beings."[3]

So I imagine that scene in the barn under the night sky, with the child in the manger, as a cosmic scene. The whole of life stands ready to take a step forward into the revelation of its very nature. Jesus's main teachings are: inclusive community, love and respect, a healing presence, release from our demonic tendencies, heartfelt friendship, and overcoming the death principle as a way of living.

This teaching, embodied in the life of the Christ, is brief and simple, like a mustard seed. But it holds the secret to the continuing evolution of our world.

Each of us is as lowly as the manger, and yet any of us could have sufficient power of vision and soul to make a huge difference in the future of this cosmos. Will our planet die out in mutual savagery, or will it become glorious because it has found a way toward peace and community?

At Christmas time don't leave out the manger. It's like a toy, a doll house, but in some ways toys are the most important inventions. Buy or make a manger and contemplate it. You are there in it. The entire universe surrounds it. Make sure there are some stars in the arrangement, because Christmas is a cosmic event. Put together the solstice background of Christmas with a Teilhardian theology of worldly spirituality and you might have an insight into the vast meaning of Christmas. You may understand how it is not limited to the Christian religion but is a view of life that must include everyone. We are, all together, growing out of this planet like walking, thinking plants, and it will take all of us together first to survive, and then to bring this life to fruition.

Our planet is about four and a half billion years old. A cultured humanity has been around for fifty thousand years. Now think about how much we have developed technologically in the past fifty years. In the scope of things, human creativity could be unimaginably effective. Of course, we'll have to develop spiritually, as well. We are not just physical beings.

So there we are in the manger, the future of the world at stake. Each of our lives is small in this grand context, but remember the mustard seed. Small is beautiful. Small is potent. It takes our small mind and small lives to push this congregation of universes to its fulfillment. The birth of Jesus is the birth of Christ, the olive oil man, who brings us to a new level of manifestation.

Another personal memory of Christmas comes to mind. One year—I suppose I was seven or eight—I got a magnificent Lionel electric model train for Christmas. My father was quite enthusiastic about it, and I have strong memories of him right next to me, literally rubbing shoulders with me, showing me how to work the large, beautiful black transformer.

What does this warm Christmas memory tell me? It reminds me of all that my parents gave me over the years. I recall how my father was always a child at heart and could play with me and not just govern my behavior. It tells me that Christmas is an opportunity for living out the Jesus teaching in small, concrete ways. If we are going to become a peaceful people, we will have to learn how to parent peacefully, and how to become parents without losing our childhood. As a therapist I know too well how often parents act out their frustrations and bad patterns with their children.

Thinking of the manger as your house, you might make it a place where angels visit and wise men travel a great distance to behold the sight, a place where the ideal is:

"Silent Night, Holy Night. All is calm; all is bright."

CHAPTER FIVE

The Guiding Star

onsider the traditional nativity scene: You can hear the animals quietly breathing and sense the quiet on the shepherds' hills. It is all earthy and intimate. But then look at the blue-black sky. It's full of wonder and takes your mind off into profound questions about the context of our lives and the meaning of it all. Now imagine a star shining with unusual brightness in that sky, apparently directly over the barn and the infant within. To get this familiar scenario, tradition has elaborated on the Gospel story, and it now brings out the drama of this extraordinary evening in the history of humankind.

Part of the Christmas story is humble and earthy, the other is cosmic and magical. Imagine angels in the thousands appearing to announce the event, and practitioners of magic far away noting a star in the night sky, a sign of an auspicious event. Both dimensions are important: the humble and the glorious. Together they help us sense the deep impact of the child on the human psyche, as well as its meaning for the destiny of the planet against the backdrop of the universe.

The star directs our attention upward to the sky, a natural symbol. You don't have to think about it but just stand in wonder at a higher, vast and mysterious world. You look at the stars at night and you can't help asking about the meaning of it all and your place in the whole, vast display. Contemplating the star of Bethlehem and the child it points to, you may ask why there was such a to-do at his birth. Why does the simple story explode with angels and a guiding star?

Jung says that the image of a child signifies renewal, a new kind of human being, and hope itself. The child may be a figure of myth, of special destiny, or even divine— which can mean having implications far beyond human understanding. The star makes the infant a cosmic child, so that even the vast universe conforms to its presence.

Remember that Jesus often speaks of his "father in the sky" and his "kingdom of the sky." The sky is a meta-phor for the infinite mysteriousness of our world. It's important to have mysteries in life. Everything shouldn't be explained. The world is partly unknowable, and may it always be so. You don't have to solve it. You may gain something by keeping the mystery and living comfort-ably with that which is out of reach of the human mind. It may be more important to wonder than to believe.

With this appreciation for mystery in mind, picture the angel appearing in the nativity scene, announcing to the shepherds that the Christos, the anointed one, has been born. An army of sky-beings, heavenly hosts, appear offering praise: "In the highest region we give honor to God, and on earth offer peace to people who are pleasing to him."

"In the highest region" could refer to the area of the stars, not literally in the sky but beyond our reach. We can think of the birth not only in historical terms but in a spiritual way. This birth has an impact on the meaning of life. Traditionally, angels speak for the spiritual realm and communicate spiritual thoughts.

When I was a child, probably around eight or nine, I used to spend several weeks of the summer on a farm in the Finger Lakes region of New York, the homestead where my relatives settled when they emigrated from Ireland in the late 1800s. I have many warm memories from those visits, but one that stands out is our habit of going to a drive-in movie in a car loaded with children. Sometimes I sat on the hood of the car and, instead of paying attention to the movie, I'd keep my eye on the dark sky. That was a perfect place to watch shooting stars, one after the other, darting across the dark palette behind the screen. I don't remember any movies that I saw at that time, but I can still envision the meteor shower that swept me away. We all need wonder as a prelude to knowledge, and few things instill wonder better than a dark sky full of movement.

This wonder-inspiring power of the night sky is the backdrop to the traditional picture of the Christ coming into the world and also the light that makes the night sky not so dark and blank. The star serves as a companion image to the solstice—light appearing in the dark. And so it is a perfect image for the spirit of Christmas, a time when we are particularly overtaken by darkness and in need of light.

In the Greek version, the narrative about the star is somewhat more mysterious and stronger than the usual

English versions. It says that the star arrived where the child was born and stood still over the place.

Of course, you can get directions from the stars at night, as navigators have done for millennia. Less literally, the star is a spiritual light telling us how we might find the place, the Bethlehem of our individual destiny, where our spiritual self will manifest.

A few years ago our family moved to a new house in the beautiful countryside of New England. Next to us on one side is a mountain, not high by the standards of the world's great mountains, but imposing and inspiring nonetheless. On the other side is a long and peaceful lake.

Right after we moved in I was startled by the joy I saw in the faces of our family members and visitors. It's a modest place, but there is the sense that it is very special. We could easily paint it with a star shining over it. We were guided to this place rather indirectly and now feel blessed to be able to enjoy it, to live our lives under that invisible but implied star. A heavenly body doesn't have to be literal to guide you where you need to go.

I felt a similar sky-omen the day I decided to leave monastic life and my long pursuit of the Catholic priesthood. For months I could feel changes happening in me, but one day I woke up with a certainty I hadn't had before. There were no good earthly reasons for me to leave that good life behind, and many of my friends thought I was making a mistake. But I felt a strong inner guidance that I knew I couldn't contradict. It was like an intelligence from another place, a light beyond my understanding and a guidepost for my life.

If I wanted to make a painting of the arc of my life, I could put a star on the spot when I was twenty-six, the day I realized I had to change directions drastically. I didn't actually see a star, but I felt one. When we consider the star of Bethlehem, we might pay more attention to the sensation of a star than to any attempt to make factual sense of it.

My poetic reading of the star takes nothing away from its importance. The star that guided me on that crucial morning was not physically visible, but it was present to my inner eye and very effective. Whether or not there was some special constellation in the year 5 BC, a star of some kind was certainly present. It is the proper omen for the cosmic event that promised to elevate humanity to a higher plane.

For my doctoral dissertation in religious studies I translated from Latin a fifteenth-century book called *De vita coelitus comparanda (Arranging Your Life to be in Tune with the Sky)* by Marsilio Ficino, a gifted man who was a magus and a theologian. He was versed in many different areas including music, theology, philosophy, language, and especially Arab writers on the magical life. In his home town of Florence in those days, there were several societies dedicated to the magi, and he belonged to one of them. They understood the three "wise men" as patrons of their own magic, by which they used music and words and letters for their power to heal and transform.

One line in his book struck me when I first read it. He says that first you should find your own star, some spiritual indicator of who you are and where you should be.

He refers to this personal star as your daimon, your inner light and guidance.

Here is yet another valuable secret to the meaning of Christmas. We shouldn't just focus on our personal needs and wishes or rely on our own intelligence as we try to live an effective life. We could look higher, beyond ourselves, and seek out a special star of guidance.

The star of Bethlehem is that kind of star. A star guided the magi to Bethlehem, and the discovery of your "star" could put you on track for your life. Eventually you may understand that you need an inner guidance that is deeper than your ordinary intelligence. You have to watch and heed that star and find your way to this child within you, who is the origin of a new vitality.

DEEP POETIC ASTROLOGICAL THINKING

Magi is the plural of *magus* and refers to one who studies secret knowledge to attain special powers. This magic may be supernatural or natural, appealing to a world beyond or tapping into certain secrets of nature that can make you more effective and productive.

A magus appreciates astrology—a meaningful charting of the planets in their orbits. Astrologers keep their eyes on the night sky and notice especially the timing of orbits and significant angles made by the planets. Today many people consider astrology as hokum or occult nonsense. It may seem superstitious and New Age. Many modern people have never considered that astrology could be deeper and less literal than the usual caricature of it. Yet, for millennia common people and leaders have lived in a world imagined through the prism of the sky, by means of a poetry based on movements always taking place in that sky. The key is to understand astrology as spiritual poetics and not fact.

We could restore the rich, old practice of finding inspiration in the poetry of the sky without superstition. We could learn from traditional astrology and yet bring a new postmodern sense of image, meaning, and synchronicity to our readings of the planets.

For myself, having studied astrology for many years, I understand it as a method for reading all events in the sky, not just the planets. Red clouds at sunset, a dramatic pink dawn, the threat of rain, ominous thunder clouds— all these manifestations in the sky can get your imagination moving in certain directions. Many people today still stop to admire a full moon or a particularly bright planet or a solar eclipse. These are natural, ordinary ways of living astrologically.

I wish we could change the name from astrology to astropoetics, because, for me at least, that is what astrology is all about. The night sky is a marvelous canvas full of moving objects on precise timetables. Looking deep into that sky we see ourselves and get hints about the laws that govern our lives. Seeing the exact arrangement of planets at the precise time of our birth, we have a symbolic picture of our essence, and throughout life we can keep coming back to that image.

If you want to pursue this way of relating to nature further, you can easily map your horoscope, noticing the position of planets at the moment you were born, and then you can track the "transits" or movements of the planets now in relation to the birth chart. Many New Testament scholars think that the magi were astrologers, and the star they were watching was either a particularly significant planet or a dramatic "aspect" of Jupiter, Saturn and Mars. My own opinion is that an astrological awareness in the storyteller led him or her to include a beautiful, simple, fairy-tale star guiding the way toward a most remarkable event.

Throughout the Gospels, Jesus is shown as someone wonderfully human and yet always connected to his "father above." It makes sense that at his birth a star, representing that world above, would be prominent and helpful. Jesus is a child of earth and heaven, and if you read the stories of his life, you will find these two directions constantly alternating: sky and earth, above and below. This is an essential ingredient of Christmas, which in many ways is an astrological festival, with its solstice calendar, Santa traversing the sky, and the theme of cosmic renewal.

A COSMIC CHRISTOS

To see Jesus as the endpoint of our evolving puts him in a cosmic panorama. The star of the magi points not only to the manger in which a special child lies, but also to the birth of our own endpoint and fulfillment. Look closely and meditatively at a Christmas manger, but don't just see a literal human baby there. See yourself in the infancy of your evolution. We are full of promise, but we need a new direction—exactly the kind that Jesus taught based on mutual love and respect. We need an end to xenophobia of all kinds, pushing far beyond legalism and moralism, and we need finally to develop a consciousness of the community of beings.

Christmas has this spirit of evolved humanity, symbolized in the gifts we give each other and the general atmosphere of kindness and well-being. In this sense, the good cheer of Christmas is not superficial but is meant to be a taste of what we could have all the time, if only we evolved further. The true meaning of Christmas is not some abstract theological belief; it's simply the spirit of giving and joy in communal life.

My own sense of purpose has evolved both consistently and unexpectedly over the years. It began when I felt the urge to become a priest and then went off in search of that goal. When I left that pursuit in my mid-twenties, I didn't know where to turn. I was in a period of rejection, having lost interest in my former goal. Then I found my way to a deeper and broader study of religion, and with the publication of my book *Care of the Soul*, suddenly I had a huge sense of purpose. I had many books to write and places to visit and the need to spell out my message.

Today I'm still aware that I am called, however you want to understand that, to speak for the soul. I'm known as a spiritual writer, and yet I have the specific mission to speak for the intimate, worldly, concrete realm of the soul as a depth aspect of spiritual development. The course of my life has led me to think globally, since people all over the world read these books, and even to imagine the cosmos in larger terms. In these ways, too, the star of Bethlehem has meaning for me. I haven't shaped my life according to my own plans but have responded to hints and indications where to go next. Like the magi, I've been following a star and pausing to go to work when that star stops at a certain point, only to move on later. I have been evolving myself and also working for the evolution of soul and spirit in the world.

Maybe we should be careful with the word *evolution*. It may imply that we will gradually improve automatically, by some natural force. But the interesting thing about human evolution is that we have a conscious role. The depth of our imagination, the capacity of our hearts to love, and our gradual learning about life and the interdependence of its parts all play an active role. We don't exactly evolve, but rather we continually create ourselves and are constantly born into new levels of understanding. The process is not automatic but depends on the generosity of our vision and our devotion to it.

The star gives image to our potentiality. It is out there in space, up and away from the earth. It is unencumbered possibility. It's a shining beacon, another world, utopia. Christmas, too, is a kind of utopian interlude set between the harsh realities of contemporary life. It's time-out, holiday, Saturnalia. It's probably best at Christmas not to try to be realistic and practical. Allow yourself some foolish celebrating, some unreal and sentimental goodness. If someone asks, say that you're following that star in the sky.

Read the Gospel of John. Although it doesn't have the story of the manger and the star, there you will hear Jesus say that he and his father above are one. When you place the star on your Christmas tree, it might be good to recite one of the lines from John, recalling that you, too, have a home among the stars, that you are a spiritual being trying to live well in a world of matter.

We are of this earth and not just living on it. If we evolve spiritually and in all other ways, the earth will evolve, too. We are all one living, conscious being. The star points to an even greater mystery: We find our way not only by our innate intelligence but by our capacity to follow a guidance that transcends us, that we sense as coming to us, being available to us, and in subtle ways "speaking" to us.

The star stands still over the place where we need to be. But we need the eyes to see that star and the special intelligence to follow it.

CHAPTER SIX

The Virgin Mother

y mother's name was Mary Virginia, and she was born on March 25th, the feast of the Annunciation, Mary becoming pregnant with a divine child. My mother prayed to the Virgin Mary all her life and was the most spiritually devout woman I've ever known. So Mary of the Christmas story has special meaning to me because in some ways I mix together the Virgin Mary and Mary Virginia, my mother.

My mother grew up in an Irish Catholic family that was warm and loving and in many ways sensual, but one that also was afraid of sex. My grandparents on my mother's side had six children, so they must have known something about sex. But my father told me once that when he got married he discovered that my mother knew next to nothing about sex. So I grew up in a confusing situation: My father was comfortable with sex, but my mother, I'm sure, never used the word.

I loved Mary Virginia. She was devout, all right, and thoroughly spiritual, but in certain areas she could be worldly. She longed for a better financial status, and she was interested as an observer in all the tangles people got into. She was also forgiving and understanding, and in spite of her strict beliefs, she would easily find a way to overlook someone's failure to live up to ideals.

I'd like to draw upon my own experience of my mother to reflect on the role of the mother in the Christmas story.

THE ANGEL AND THE BOOK

It begins with the annunciation. An awesome angel appears to a young unmarried woman to tell her that she is pregnant by a mysterious heavenly fatherhood, by "a holy spirit" and "a power from on high." The child to be born, the "holy being" in the original Greek, would be a son of God.

Paintings show Mary in an enclosed garden, a symbol of her virginity. Sometimes she is reading a book when the angel shows up. This detail has long prompted me to make reading a major activity in my life when I want to be open to something special developing in me. Although reading is not in the Gospel story of the annunciation, it's so common in paintings that I see it as an essential part of becoming spiritually "pregnant."

I don't read much for information. Well, I do a lot of research that entails tracking down ideas and the history of words, but when I really read I'm reading to be inspired. In fiction or biography, I observe how people express their emotions, follow their fate, resolve problems and heroically accomplish great things. Through reading, I'm inspired to live my own life with courage and adventure.

I also read poetry, loving a good turn of phrase or a perfectly chosen word. I appreciate good translations and particularly enjoy creative use of language. I appreciate my namesake Thomas More's feeling that wit is the mother of thought. If some new life possibility is going to be born in me, it will probably happen when I'm reading.

In one of my favorite paintings of the scene, by Jacques Yverni in the National Gallery of Ireland, a tall lily plant stands between Mary and the angel. As already mentioned, you often see some kind of barrier between them showing the curtain between the realm of high spirit and the lowly human. In addition, the lily symbolizes her virginity. Mary is also standing in an architectural framework, adding to the separation between her and the angel. And she's reading a book.

As an aside, paintings are a good source of theological reflection. You can read definitions and long descriptions in books, but paintings can offer subtle nuances that address the imagination and not just the rational mind. The imagination is closer to our emotions, and it doesn't thrive on precise definitions as much as soft hints at the hidden elements in a teaching. For example, when I study many paintings of angels I have strong images of what angels do and what they are essentially. I feel drawn to them and want to see more images of angels so that I can understand better what they are all about.

We can't have the Christmas birth, even if it's spiritual in nature, without the conception. Some say that in this scene Mary is a virgin because her child is destined for a greater-than-human future. He requires a supernatural or at least an extraordinary conception and birth. Tradition says that his mother, like the mothers of many heroes and legendary figures, is a virgin.

My mother, Mary Virginia, passed on a considerable amount of Catholic guilt and anxiety to me that is an annoyance even today, but she also gave me an early model of contemplation and mysticism. She was a simple, ordinary woman, and yet I believe she was a mystic. She was so developed and shaped by her devotion that her entire life and personality sparkled with it. I don't know how I could have become a spiritual person and written my books without her. Even as a child I knew that she was at home among the angels.

It's difficult to put into words exactly how sexuality defined as spiritual plays out in life. I felt it as a monk living in an intensely spiritual community. People would ask how I could I could be celibate in my late teens and early twenties. I didn't know just how to answer, but I vaguely understood that the thoroughness of my dedication to a spiritual way of life somehow satisfied my sexual needs. When presented with the question, I would immediately think of the community I loved, knowing somehow that I could fulfill my sexuality through the joy of that utopian, radically communal way of living.

Sex is not just about physical touch, as important as that is. It's also found in living radically from the heart: caring deeply for others, sharing possessions, and finding yourself fulfilled in the well-being of your friends. If that is so, then Christmas is also a commemoration of this mystery where complete sex is somehow virginal. You keep yourself intact, and yet you connect more intimately than otherwise possible. Not being part of a couple, you are freer to give yourself to a community.

Obviously the birth of a child may fulfill your sexuality. It is not essential, but it may be part of sexual love. Annunciation, a divine experience of sexuality, leads to

Christmas—the birth of a divine child, one who can work miracles and transform the world. Taking the whole mystery in a spiritual way, it means that each of us can respond to an invitation "from above" and give birth to a spiritual personality who can accomplish great things.

THE ARCHANGEL GABRIEL

Let's return to the scene of the enclosed garden. Mary, again as in many paintings, is quietly reading her book. She is prepared, thoughtful, educated. The great archangel appears. If you are not a believer of any kind, think of this as spiritual poetry. The story goes that the great infinity that surrounds our lives, full of mystery, peeks through at times. We glimpse it. It has messengers who reveal its truths: angels. A few of these messengers are primary, tremendous in their glory, and Gabriel is one of them.

Gabriel appears in religious history at important times, as when he interprets a dream for Daniel or reveals spiritual insights to Mohammed. But this annunciation is his biggest job of all: asking the woman to become a mother in a miraculous and mysterious manner. He tells her:

A holy spirit will come over you
and power from above will envelope you in shadow
and the holy being to be born
will be called a son of God. (Luke 1:35)

At that moment Mary conceived a unique and mysterious thing. The Greek uses a neuter word, an "it" rather than a "him." Not just a person, but a being like none other. A phenomenon. I sometimes imagine Jesus as being from another planet, but that is only my way of trying to appreciate his otherworldliness. The other side of him is his deep humanity. In the early centuries theologians were at pains to keep this oxymoron of the divine and the human intact.

Annunciation is one of the most important stories ever told. It describes how at certain moments each of us may be invited to incarnate, in our own small spheres, a larger purpose. Incarnation means giving flesh to. To in-carnate (*carnis* = flesh, as in "carnal"). Life gives body to spirit, and spirit gives purpose to life. Human beings are the vessels in which incarnation takes form, because annunciation happens whenever we feel inspired or invited to entertain and embody some wonderful idea. We call it a conception, as in "I conceived an idea for a new business." But we don't usually think of it as a spiritual impregnation.

The angel—the messenger and the message, connecting the highly spiritual with the ordinarily human—tells the woman that she will become pregnant and that the father will be a holy spirit. The child will be human and yet other than human, both "him" and "it." The spiritual joins with mundane life, and the encounter results in a new kind of being: worldly and yet otherworldly, earthly and yet heavenly, physical and yet spiritual.

The mother, capable of containing these mysteries and paradoxes, has been honored for centuries as the necessary partner of the divine in this sublime theological event. She is a virgin and a mother, not in the physical sense, but in her being. When we are spiritually impregnated, we become more intact, more who we are. For example, when I heard the message that day in the monastery and knew that I had to leave for a different way of life, I was invited to be more myself: my psyche more virginal, not less. I would be more identified with myself and less with an institution, and that is a form of psychological virginity.

This mother is unique: According to tradition, she is immaculately conceived, which means that from the first moment of her existence she was free of any taint of human moral imperfection; at her death she was also taken up into the sky—"assumed" is the technical term. She has her place above the normal and the merely human. She is rightfully among the angels and other great spiritual beings. If she were associated with a different religion, she'd be considered a goddess.

Remember that here we are speaking theologically, or mythologically if you like, and not medically or physically. We can have our own experience of annunciation and Christmas by being open to a spiritual transformation in the form of an inner pregnancy. At Christmas you can meditate on how you have been pregnant with spiritual possibilities. Now is the time for fruition—time to give birth to yourself or to an aspect of your soul.

BARBELO, THE SPHERE OF THE MOTHER

Recent biblical scholarship has offered us excellent editions of ancient Gospels that were not part of the official canon or accepted list. This doesn't mean they are objectionable in any way but that they have to be read in context. Understanding that they are not the strictly accepted theology, we can still find inspiration and fresh ways of imagining the beauty of the Christmas message.

The Gospel I'm about to explore briefly introduces a word and idea that were around in the time of Jesus and gave a positive, feminine background to what is usually presented as entirely masculine. I mention this somewhat obscure idea here because I think it adds a beautiful dimension to the Christmas story.

I like spiritual mysteries and words that convey mysteries mysteriously. One of the best appears in the Gospel of Judas, published to some acclaim not long ago. At a crucial point in Judas's story, this apostle known only as the betrayer exclaims that he knows who Jesus is: "You are from Barbelo," he says. I imagine him shouting this with great passion.

Barbelo is the mysterious word. In Gnostic thinking, it lies at the origins of life, not biologically but theologically, as the realm of the Great Mother, the condition in which all things come into existence and are nurtured. It is the realm of all mothers imagined as a special plane of existence.

I picture Barbelo as a special sphere of life surrounded by a thin bubble of plasma. You can come and go through this plasma, but, thin as it is and so transparent that you don't see that you're entering it, when you're there everything in life has reference to the mothers.

I feel it often when I'm practicing therapy. The man or woman in front of me feels tender and raw. I know they're going through a powerful, challenging experience. Sometimes there are hints of suicide, the transformation is so difficult. I allow myself to pass through the plasma of the mother, if only briefly, to bring the compassion I feel into the setting. I don't want to stay there, because the mother stuff can be overwhelming in its own way.

It's possible to be too compassionate. Still, I want regular access to Barbelo. That is where Jesus comes from, Judas says. I feel Jesus's connection to Barbelo in his frequent and deep expressions of care.

The Barbelo aspect of Christmas, the presence of the woman who becomes a special kind of mother, is essential, and we really don't grasp the meaning of Christmas without it. From annunciation to nativity, the mother spirit is strong, and we, participating in this mystery, not just observing it, have to pass through Barbelo ourselves, feeling in our being what it means to be thoroughly maternal. The great mystic Julian of Norwich referred to Jesus as mother. She must have had a mystical intuition of his Barbelo nature.

My own mother was immersed in motherhood. She seemed to have originated in Barbelo as well, and maybe that's why she was such an ardent follower of Jesus. She gathered herself into a massive motherly cloud for her children, but also for many other people she encountered and didn't know as well. Her compassion leapt out of her without any hesitant thought to slow it down.

Again we can think about Christmas customs and see Barbelo in the background, especially the gift-giving and the food and the hospitality of the season. This is the matrix of Jesus, his originating plasma that saturated everything he did. And so it is central, like seed stuff, at Christmas.

A MYSTICAL CHRISTMAS

Christmas offers an opportunity to get in touch with your own mystical side. We are all potential mystics. Just stand still in the presence of a beautiful sunset and your mysticism will be activated. An essential ingredient is wonder and the capacity to become absorbed, to lose yourself for moment in wonder or contemplation.

Meditate on the nativity scene in your town or neighborhood. Have one in your home, whatever your spiritual preferences are. Don't take it lightly. Nothing could be more important than finding ways to incorporate in your person and your life the moment when the spiritual realm fully intersects with your ordinary life.

You may feel that there is no room for you in the inn of religion or community or tradition. That's an appropriate feeling for this time. Find your own stable, your humble place in the world. Let the revelation happen. Listen for the angels announcing the good news that another life has been redeemed and transformed.

At Christmas time we can all discover the Christos in us and the Virgin Mary as well—the maternal, feminine, mystical figure who can say yes to life. Imitating Mary, you say, "Let it be. Let me be the vessel. I don't know what it's all about, but if it furthers life, I am willing. I want to be the means by which human life advances."

But you don't become a mystic by wishing it so. There's work to do. You need some quiet time, some contemplation, some meditation, some deprivation and some deep prayer. You don't have to be a Christian or a member of any religion to do these things. I always remember my Renaissance teacher Ficino saying that religion is as natural to a human being as barking is to a dog. You can be a natural, ordinary and unaligned mystic.

The mystical life has some quiet in it. Notice I'm not suggesting silence, though silence has its place. Quiet can be the atmosphere you create; not all the time, of course, but at moments when it's convenient and possible. The goal is not to be successful in calming your speech and your thoughts—mysticism is not a hero's way. The idea is to create an environment in which you can reflect and can listen to what the world has to say to you. You become quiet to be a good listener.

In our home I cherish the quiet times, especially in early morning and late evening. There's a lot going on in between. These times place a quality of peace on the whole day and create an atmosphere conducive to spiritual experiences.

As a monk I particularly appreciated the visual quiet of the monastery. I mean that the materials and colors and images of the buildings helped create the atmosphere in which spiritual things had a home. The massive wood doors were effective spiritually more than physically. They kept the meaning of the interior monastery intact. In our home now we don't have massive doors, though I would like them. One of our houses in the past had reclaimed monastery doors. But today we have a longish curving driveway up to the house from the narrow dirt road, and that helps to give the house its interiority and spiritual usefulness.

We've always had meditation rooms and altars in our house. I remember on an early trip to Ireland visiting a well-preserved old castle and seeing a beautiful side chapel built into a corner tower. It gave me the idea of always having a room for spirit. Maybe you can see how making your home a place of spirit echoes the mother at the manger in gentle repose.

I find some contemplative moments at Christmas time listening to special pieces of music, such as J.S. Bach's "Christmas Oratorio." Decades ago a highly cultured monk taught me to appreciate medieval carols, and I still sing and play them every Christmas. One year I joined up with Scottish fiddle player Johnny Cunningham to produce a recording of Christmas music with an Irish lilt. My family can't seem to get through the Christmas season without listening to that set of songs many times.

I would also recommend contemplating a painting of the annunciation that appeals to you. There are hundreds, each offering a slight variation on the theme. Remember that a painting is not a simple representation of an idea or historical event but an evocation of the mystery involved. Contemplating a painting can be one of the most effective ways to cultivate your personal mysticism. In this case, I'm suggesting that we take the theme of Barbelo, the deep mystery of the mothers, and make that our Christmas focus.

Another maternal way to enter into contemplation is to go into nature with a child. Young children see the world in their own way, and as you contemplate a garden or river or mountain, or watch animals living their lives, in the company of a child, you may gain some of the outlook of Barbelo and foster the deep spiritual mothering that is so important to the spiritual life and that plays a central role at Christmas.

CHAPTER SEVEN

The Christmas Tree

very year in North America and Europe at Christmas time people buy over one hundred million Christmas trees and bring them into their homes. Obviously this is not a practical decision. Who needs a tree in all its natural glory standing in the center of their living room? It only makes sense as a ritual act, one that has symbolic meaning.

If you ask someone why they have a tree in their house, they probably will be hard-pressed to come up with a good answer. It's just what people do, what they grew up with and what they want to pass on to their children. Each year magazines and newspapers contain articles explaining the history of the Christmas tree, but rarely do they explore the mysteries and the truly serious meaning of this festival. They don't tell you why you should bring a tree into your living room.

The Christmas tree, so simple and yet so strange, is a natural symbol that speaks to many people without elaborate explanation. It was there, you remember it, you know it was meaningful, even if you can't put that meaning into words. The lights and ornaments made you happy. You knew that Christmas was a special time, though you have never heard about liminality, utopia, or soul and spirit.

My father, who loved buying and installing the family tree, would usually pick out one with ugly gaps in it. He would drill holes in the trunk and stick branches in them to make the tree look fuller and then string wires from the trunk to the wall to keep the tree upright. For him the Christmas tree was a production, and my memories of his efforts are still poignant and funny. He was a loving man who adored children, no more so than at Christmas, and he put himself into making it all perfect.

One year in my childhood my Uncle Jack, who was the artist in the greater family, painted some stiff paper a bluish-gray color, making mountains to set up behind the stable at the foot of the tree. I would lie on the floor and gaze for a long time at those mountains and imagine the nativity story playing out. I'm sure my uncle couldn't have explained liminality, but he took his job seriously. He was doing what we all should do at Christmas—enter the spirit, decorate the house, buy good gifts, and make the nativity scene beautiful.

The rituals of Christmas are truly rituals, part of the holy festival. They should be done with care. Ritual feeds the soul the way food nourishes the body. But good ritual needs imagination, care, and time. It's worth your effort to find stunning nativity figures or simple crafted ones and special ornaments for the tree. The more you put into it, the more the ritual will affect you.

The stable with its shepherds, animals, the baby, and his parents is simple and yet so profound. As you set up your nativity scene, your fantasy may take you away into wonder: Why was Jesus born in a barn? Should I take those hosts of angels seriously? Why shepherds? Why not a bunch of theologians?

As a child, of course, I was interested in the fairy tale of the baby lying in the manger and visited by wise men. I didn't yet know about the philosophy of the Christos and the human search for utopia, for a world of peace, beauty and love. And only much later would I see how this celebration could have meaning to someone wishing for a better world.

Children are especially charmed by the nativity scene. Families play their part, too, going out and looking for the perfect tree, debating the merits of one over the other, tying it to the roof of the car and bringing it into the house—this is all strong ritual. People speak vaguely about spirituality, but this is the real thing.

Then unwrapping the small carved statues of Mary, Joseph, the magi and the other figures from storage, placing them in the just the right spots, attaching the star or angel onto the top of the tree: these acts show a basic reverence that is part of natural religion and piety. Especially in our world—where we neglect the role of ritual, sacred speech, contemplative actions, poetry, symbol and myth—the simple rites of Christmas bring us back to a symbolic way of life.

Ritual is something you do with your body. There are actions, objects and sounds involved. You may not think of setting up a tree and the crib as ritual, but it reaches far deeper into the psyche than would appear. Especially for children and family members, nothing could be more nutritious for their souls than to engage in rituals that delight.

Children look to their parents to explain, once again, what this odd story of the birth in a barn is all about. Why did the magi, magicians and astrologers make an arduous trip to see this infant? Because he was God? No, that theology came much later. Something much more mysterious was clearly in play.

What is the star doing at the top of the tree? To begin with, it directs our gaze upward, to the sky, which, as we've seen, plays a central role in the Christmas story, the Jesus teaching, and the solstice celebration. We see the star and think cosmos, fate, and mystery.

Today we tend to value interpretation over ritual action. We like to explain everything. But recent theories about images place more emphasis on your deportment in the presence of images and their ritual context than on interpretation. It may be more important to create an impressive nativity scene than to explain all its elements.

People of the past might respond to an image or teaching with music and dance, treating images as real presences. In many places people place flowers and food around statues of the deities or other holy figures. We tend to judge such behavior as "animism," and we consider it primitive and deluded. But maybe there is something of value in that approach, something which we've sadly lost.

I am not suggesting that we go back to animism or a naive view of reality, but I do think we can and need to move past the exclusive rationalism of the modern era toward some new consciousness where we can still enjoy our scientific knowledge but also honor images directly. Think of it as a kind of postmodern approach or a new animism or neo-animism; a more sophisticated way of allowing images a presence in and of themselves, without definitions and explanations.

This profound philosophical issue applies to the simple act of putting together a nativity scene beneath the tree, keeping alive an imagination of the sacred. The tree supplies some ritual activity that helps sanctify one of the most important days of the year. And it keeps Christmas in the realm of a sacred and serious work or play of imagination.

THE COSMIC TREE

The Christmas tree is not in the Gospel story, but the idea of a sacred tree is common throughout the world. In India people place ribbons and flowers on trees considered sacred. Scandinavians used to honor a special version of the world tree called Yggdrasil, a tree whose roots go down so deep in the earth that no one could know how far. At its top stands an eagle and around its bottom coils a snake.

Closer to the Jesus birth story is the Paradise Tree, the tree that stood in the center of Eden and the tree that plays a central role in the fate of Adam and Eve. Scholars refer to it as the "Cosmic Tree." Later spiritual poets connected the Paradise Tree with the tree of Golgotha, the cross on which Jesus was executed.

While these interesting references are not direct links to the Christmas tree, they help us understand how a tree could become central in a sacred ritual. It is not just a tree of nature to be enjoyed for its physical properties; it is also a tree of a sanctifying imagination, a tree that helps mark the sacred dimension of the winter solstice and the story of Jesus.

Every year my wife and daughter go away to celebrate the winter solstice in their Sikh community. This year they got home on December 23, leaving us one day to find a tree. We decided to cut down a tree on the land around our house. We found two possibilities: one was a perfectly formed pine tree, but it was about ten feet wide at its base and the trunk was massive. It was also about twelve feet tall. The other was a thin, scrawny tree full of gaps and having very weak branches. I favored the anorexic tree, and that's the one we cut down.

I thought lights and ornaments would cover up all the tree's defects, but they only accented them. The decorated tree reminded me of the medieval fool with tufted cap and rubbery body. Still, we developed affection for this tree, as you might for any human being displaying imperfection.

In fact, a tree is much like a person. Picture a tree standing majestically on the horizon. Horizontally, the cosmic tree is the center of the world and therefore marks a place of exceptional power. Now imagine the tree's verticality. It reaches high into the air and its roots penetrate deep into the earth, joining the world above with the world below. Many also see a tree as an abstract human form, as though it were a human standing on the earth. So the Christmas tree, an echo of the Tree of Paradise and of Golgotha and Yggdrasil, connects our daily realm with what is above and below, the general goal of all spiritual rites.

Look at the tree and imagine its roots going down into the vast underworld and its top extending into the heavens. Put a star or angel on its top; both are appropriate, and both signify the heavens, the realm of spirit. At the bottom place the crib—humble, earthly, human. The Christmas tree teaches with its silent presence that the season has to do not just with the fate of the Earth but with the whole of the universe. See Yggdrasil in it, with the eagle/angel on top and the serpent at the bottom. Right here in your home is the cosmic tree, the great, worldwide image for the whole of life, both highly spiritual and deeply rooted. And that great tree of the imagination stands rooted in everyday life.

Shamans sometimes paint the world tree on their drums, charting various levels of reality they traverse. You might see this tree of visionary, mystical travel in pagodas and church spires, somewhat abstract and figurative. If you really use your imagination, you might see it in skyscrapers that try in their own way to embrace several layers of reality: a livable middle, a mind-altering height, and the invisible depths in the earth where basic shopping, parking and engineering take place.

Another aspect of the Christmas tree that many people comment on is its fragrance. You bring it into your house, and it may give off that special aroma of earth and tree and nature. Fragrance speaks directly to the soul, often giving rise to memories of Christmases past and family members and good times. Or, it may only offer a feeling of freshness and purity. You may not know what the fragrance is all about, and yet you enjoy it as part of Christmas.

Scent is important because, as I keep emphasizing, ritual is an experience of the body and of objects and their qualities. My Catholic childhood comes back to me at the smell of incense, beeswax and wine, used in the liturgy. Some people might associate Christmas with the smells of food. I think of turkey cooking in the kitchen of my grandmother's house and the infinitesimal whiff of Mogen David wine allowed to us children on Christmas.

We add more symbolism to the tree when we decorate it with ornaments. Exquisite glass globes, some of them very ordinary and inexpensive, are full of symbolic implications. Look up the painting "Salvator Mundi" by Leonardo da Vinci that has recently been verified and notice that Jesus holds a glass sphere in his hand, an image of the universe, the same shape as a Christmas ornament. "Salvator Mundi" means "savior of the world" It also could be "The One Who Transformed the Universe." We could easily see the entirety of the world as a glass orb, and it is that world that concerns us at Christmas.

One of the most imaginative and brilliant of Renaissance theologians was Nicolas of Cusa, who quotes an old saying: "God is an infinite sphere, whose center is everywhere, and whose circumference is nowhere."[4] Those little glass globes we hang on our Christmas trees embody this mystery. God is nowhere and everywhere at the same time. He is everything and nothing. He is a sphere, a glass orb. He is what we know and love, and yet is utterly unknowable. For many mystics, like Nicolas, the emptiness the atheist sees is exactly what God is.

At Christmas we celebrate this mystery. Of course there's no room in the inn for such an impenetrable phenomenon. We can't fit it into our knowable world. It's like the tree we bring into our homes at the solstice time. It is utterly inappropriate. It makes sense only as a bizarre piece of poetry.

The Christmas tree is a wondrous ritual object in a world that has lost its genius for ritual. It is a symbol that we take into our homes and enjoy and to which we give a place of honor. We also put it in our city squares and in our government centers. How wonderful that we still enjoy some small talent for animism, for images that are expressive and for poetic statements that give meaning to life.

One final note: There is no reason why anyone— atheist, Buddhist, Christian, Native American, Jew— cannot appreciate and take to heart this tree of life. It speaks to us as humans, not as members of any partic- ular religion or tradition. Just as anyone might be spiritu- ally enriched by Buddhist meditation and by Kabbalistic symbolism, anyone can put a Christmas tree in his home and benefit from its rich spiritual meaning. The tree is not solely Christian; it belongs to the world.

CHAPTER EIGHT

Angels in the Sky

Imagine a dark, starry night on the outskirts of a small town, shepherds watching out for their sheep, when suddenly, out of the stillness, a bright and shining being from another reality altogether appears and tells you to go and see a baby that has just been born in a barn. Then a massive army of these strange, impressive beings appears and together tell you that this event that has just happened is awesome and of great importance for humanity. This is the story of nativity presented in the second chapter of the Gospel of Luke.

These visitors, angels, are not from another planet but from another order altogether. Thomas Aquinas, the great medieval philosopher, called them "separate beings." They are real but not of the world that we know and understand. They exist in a separate reality.

The sky where these beautiful but strange beings appear is not just air or space. We experience it, our imaginations in full gear, as a realm where angels and spirits, gods and goddesses, and God have their abode. Try to grasp this: The sky is one thing to the scientific imagination but quite another to the spiritual imagination. Mention God, and many people will look up into the sky. Stand in a field at night looking up into the canopy of stars above you, and you will likely be transported and think of many things that matter, like your smallness and your future and the meaning of it all. The sky has special power to turn our minds in a certain direction, and there we find angels.

Because angels live in another world or at another level, we don't usually see them with our eyes but sense their presence from their impact on life.

A few years ago I was driving in Hartford, Connecticut, in an area I didn't know well. I was on a multilane broad street and didn't see the stop sign far off on the side. I thought I had the right of way and drove into an intersection. A massive cement truck made a turn into my path, the driver not thinking about traffic because he had the right of way. I pushed my foot hard on the brake pedal in my small coupe, and the car kept moving toward the truck. I was sure I would be hit, and I would be tiny blue David to the red truck Goliath. Somehow we didn't collide. I have no idea why I escaped that certain accident, but a theologically minded person might say that my guardian angel was sitting beside me that day.

We modern sophisticates think we know what is real and what is not. If we can kick it, it's real. If not, it's imaginary or delusional. We are quick to label another person's perceptions insane. Angels are for naive believers. But this narrow modernism is slowly giving way to a new era that some simply call post-modern. I think the next age might be the era of the imagination, in which we take seriously imaginal figures like angels without confusing them for actual beings. We will know how to tell the difference.

One day when I four years old, I was out on a big lake in a small boat with my grandfather. I have photos of other occasions when he had taken me to fish or just row. This day the winds came up and capsized the boat, and my grandfather held me up out of the water. I still remember the events quite well, and I can still feel his arms under me, holding me against the underside of the overturned boat.

I have a newspaper clipping that tells the story in an oddly cool narrative.

"The grandfather held the boy above his head as he struggled to keep afloat. The grandfather, exhausted by his efforts, cried out for help. Persons in a passing boat managed to pick up all three (my uncle swam out to try to rescue us) but two hours' work failed to revive the grandfather."

This is one of the defining episodes in my life, my first real encounter with death and my first taste of an older man giving so much to me. But notice how the newspaper account puts it: "Persons in a passing boat managed to pick up all three." My grandfather kept me from drowning but persons in a passing boat brought me to safety. If you read the story closely, you may conclude that these persons, though people in the flesh, were angels doing their work on my behalf. Angels often appear out of nowhere at just the right time.

Of course, it was my grandfather's fate, God's will, that his life end and mine in a way resurrect. Angels do the will of God and serve a person's destiny.

I don't talk about angels in my daily life, but when I read about them in the Gospels or look at paintings of them making music or giving announcements, I take them seriously and I look closely to see exactly what they look like and what they are doing. They appear in many different religious traditions, giving them considerable weight.

At Christmas time we sing about angels, and it might be worth our time to listen closely to what we say: "Angels we have heard on high." We see and hear them in the sky. Irish stories sometimes compare angels and birds. A monk notices birds lined up on a tree in the monastery garden, and later he discovers that they were angels. The angels of Christmas come out of that vast expanse of sky that evokes a sense of another world and eternal time. Angels serve the deity, the absolute, the nameless other in relation to which we pursue our lives.

The basis for taking angels seriously is to remember that the issues that religion and spirituality explore are beyond full human understanding. They are mysteries— unsolvable but crucial realities that touch upon our happiness. The only way to move close to them is through the imagination and an imagistic, poetic form of expression. The reality that an angel points to is the most serious aspect of human life. The image of an angel best describes what is going on. But if you take the image literally or physically, you miss the whole point. A sophisticated spiritual way of life requires, absolutely, an appreciation for images. And Christmas is full of them.

The Gospel story of the birth of Jesus tells of an angel who announces the event to shepherds out in the fields, followed by the appearance of a great of number of angels offering praise. They give the simple birth setting spiritual grandeur with their impressive display. They place the event within the realm of spiritual evolution, not historical fact. These angels are real, and they are important. We should keep talking about them. But we don't have to think of them as people with wings. They are of a different order, and it would be better if we could come to appreciate their world instead of dismissing them because they don't fit into ours.

Angel Music

Musicians will tell you that they can only play effectively when they are "in the zone." They have to find a way outside of normal self-consciousness and allow some other level of reality take over. I feel this way when I play the piano, which is almost every morning when I'm home. I have to let the music take me away so there isn't much thinking between me and the keyboard. That's why I say quite seriously that the piano is one of my major instruments of meditation. I don't meditate much when I am just sitting, but I do meditate when I am sitting on the piano bench.

What is being in the zone other than finding another level of reality where magic happens? The angels of Christmas appear in a similar "zone." They have an impact on earthly life, and yet they are not quite of it. They are separate. So I wonder if the reason we find carols and other Christmas music so prominent throughout the world at this time of year has to do with the angels of Christmas. Music is their form of expression and communication. For years I've looked at paintings of angel musicians playing all sort of instruments and singing in choirs, and

I've wondered if all music is the work of angels. When we sing, do we conjure up the angels and hear their important messages in their own language—song? Remember that the very word *angel* means either "message" or "messenger." Even the word *gospel*, from a Greek word *eu-angelon*, means "good message" or "good angel."

Another way to put it, one that I feel comfortable with, is that Christmas music speaks to the soul. It creates an atmosphere that is Christmas. At a shopping mall you may hear a carol, and you know that you're in the realm of Christmas. It's like hearing French spoken in Paris. You know where you are because of the language you hear everywhere.

"Hark! The Herald Angels Sing." Listen to the one who announces an important event, the herald. Here it's a host of angels. Or, "Sing, choirs of angels. Sing in exultation." Angels express our wonder and awe at the vast significance of Christmas. Angels speak for us because they are the experts at expressing feelings and thoughts that go beyond anything reasonable. They help us stretch our capacity to understand and express our response to what is happening.

Twenty years ago, along with several Irish and Scottish musicians, I produced an album of Christmas music. We worked for months throughout the hot summer in a studio in mid-Manhattan overdubbing part after part of music that gave a Celtic accent to the familiar carols. That project meant a great deal to me, in large part because of the ideas I'm presenting here. I wanted to conjure up the angels in the middle of summer to create through music the very atmosphere of Christmas. I wanted to serve the angels as they do their important part in making Christmas palpable and absorbing.

THE ANGEL AS GO-BETWEEN

Traditionally angels are go-betweens, connecting the invisible and sublime realm of the divine with our human lives. One of their jobs is to convey messages from the spiritual world to human beings. But they have other tasks as well, such as protecting, guiding, announcing and praising. Paintings often show them playing musical instruments and speaking while their words float around them on banners.

Angels have wings because they move wonderfully between realms of fact, spiritual vision, and poetic under-standing. They speak, often at first comforting their human contact with words such as "Don't be afraid." In paintings their words are often written on scrolls, empha-sizing the style of their words, a mediation from above to below. You can think of a muse as a kind of angel, who, figuratively speaking, whispers subtle ideas into your ears.

So at the birth of Jesus an angel appears to the shep-herds and explains to them and to us what is taking place.

> The angel said to them, "Don't be afraid. I bring you a wonderful, joyful message intended for all people. Today in the city of David was born someone who will deliver you. He is anointed with oil, Christos, a master from the house of David.
>
> Here is what you should look for: a baby wrapped in bands of fabric and lying in a feeding trough."
> Suddenly with the angel there appeared a huge army of angels praising God:

"Glory to God high above

And here on earth

peace to people

of compassion." (Luke 2:14)

The most sophisticated among us can take this message to heart. First, let's set aside our fears and small ideas at Christmas and have courage as we hear about the birth of a new kind of human being. The message is joyful and is intended for all people, not just a particular group.

There is a teaching that can deliver us, free us, from those mindsets and habits of behavior that take away the pure joy of life and destroy community. The teacher is archetypal, a spiritual being, anointed with oil, a Christos, as we each can be. Just as people speak of having the Buddha Nature, you can have the Christos, or if you prefer, the Christ Nature. The oil signifies, as I have already described, how we can step up to a new evolved way of being instead of remaining unconscious and acting out our frustrations and residual anger.

The army of angels offers honor to God above and peace to people on earth who have compassion. As above, so below, as the ancient saying goes. When we say "above," we are once again evoking the sky metaphor that is so prominent in the Christian festival. In every detail the Christmas story presents and links the high spiritual realm with familiar life on Earth.

The angels wish peace for people who, in the original Greek, are pleasing, who present themselves as good. I translate it somewhat freely as people with compassion because the people you want around you are compassionate. To call them "pleasant" would be too weak. They please because they have good feelings toward people. That is probably the thought behind the common translation, "peace to men of good will."

One of the basic tasks of a human being is to find ways to be spiritual and worldly at the same time. One good way is to be very human and very idealistic as you wish for peace among people. Any marked separation between these two realms usually causes trouble. If you're too spiritual, you may hurt your family and friends, have trouble with your sexuality, and fail to give enough attention to making a living and enjoying life. If you're too worldly, you may not have the great vision needed to be happy and creative and contribute to humanity. Your values may be too self-centered, and your sense of purpose weak and limited. We all need both a strong spiritual center and a love of life. Spirit and soul.

Christmas is one of several festivals in the world that honor the attempt to get spirit and ordinary life together. Theologians call it "incarnation," giving spirit a body and human context. Jesus is born into human life, sent as a messenger himself. He has angel properties, signs of the spirit world above even as he embraces life on earth. Maybe this is his greatest source of attraction to people: he is obviously both very human and very spiritual, very much a real person in this lower realm but also at home in the world above.

Jesus works miracles, as we say, exhibiting his otherworldly nature, his origin from above. When we get this dual realm in place, we, too, are capable of extraordinary things. Holiness is not just about being saintly and good, but also about having real power, especially the power to heal. Even for a doctor this power is sometimes miraculous.

It's entirely appropriate, therefore, that angels appear at the birth. They are the ones assigned to move between the world above and the world below. In sacred art, they have beautiful bodies and often have great wings. They are communicators in language and music. They break through the thin veil that keeps these realms separate. Sometimes their wings are even used to protect and conceal the secret of the world above or the presence of divinity. You can't break that veil with impunity without care and assistance. The shaman will tell you all about the dangers in too freely approaching the intensity of the spiritual realm. It takes a special kind of being, an angel, or the assistance of an angel.

Some of our greatest poets have taken angels seriously. Rainer Maria Rilke wrote about the angel as revealing the secrets of life. Wallace Stevens alluded to the "necessary angel"—who says, "in my sight you see the earth again."[5] You see what has been invisible, taken too literally. Anne Sexton also wrote about angels, especially about the earthiness with which they intrude upon our lives.

These are not naive, literalistic, or sentimental comments on angels. Only a person who has really lived life and who has suffered can speak properly of angels, because with their special position between heaven and earth they can offer us the fullness of life. Only someone who has a profound interior experience of the spiritual can refer to an angel as a personal companion.

And that is what Christmas is all about—the gift of life, suggested in the gifts we give to our loved ones. Human life can reach its fullness only when it is lived as much above as below, when it incarnates, blending a great vision with a sensuous embrace of earthly life.

CHAPTER NINE

The Coming of the Magi

good story like the one of the nativity of Christ is like a snowball on a hill. As it rolls down through history it gains in mass and fantasy. That's what happened to the story of the magi who came from the east (or the land of the rising sun) to give honor to the child. Tradition gave the magi a number. We think of three of them, though the Gospel doesn't specify. We even have names for them, though there are no names in the Gospel. Over time, they became the source of great fascination and were part of the popular and highly respected festival of Epiphany—the showing or revelation.

The word *magus*, the singular of magi, has become important to me ever since the day in graduate school when I found my dissertation topic. I was in the music section of the library at Syracuse University desperate for a good topic on which to spend a year doing research and writing. I should have been in the world religion section, since religion was my major. But I found myself in the music area when I happened to look up high on the stacks and saw a shelf of black faux-leather covered volumes. On my toes, I reached up and randomly pulled down one of the books, opening it in the middle. I found an article on Marsilio Ficino, a fifteenth-century priest and philosopher who started a movement placing soul at the heart of culture, and who based his highly original work on his studies of Plato, music, astrology, and magic. Magic!

I decided I'd write about this man and his quirky ideas. He hadn't been translated into English, so I thought I could work on his Latin, explain his ideas for our time, and do a proper dissertation. I figured I'd polish him off in a year and get on with my life. But the way it turned out, Ficino has been at the center of my life and my work ever since. Every book I've written is to some extent a comment on Ficino's special vision for humanity. To me it's an inspiring one, and it all centers around what Ficino called "natural magic."

For Ficino, magic is the ability to tap into the power in the natural world and in made things with human ingenuity. It's not rational or mechanical power, but a mystifying ability to accomplish things through what is largely secret knowledge.

For example, one of Ficino's later followers, Abbot Trithemius, was drawn to the magic power of words. Remember that this is natural magic and quite ordinary, for all its power. Think of the potency in words like "I love you" or "I do." These words don't just convey meaning, they strike with considerable impact on a person's life. Consider the words "We the People" or "We have nothing to fear but fear itself." Words can have power in the right context, phrased in a certain manner and spoken with emotion. This is ordinary magic.

In all my work as a therapist, writer and speaker, I have been aware of this natural magic and I have tried to both use it and teach it. So when I read in the Gospel of Matthew that magi came to honor Jesus, I take note. I know already that Jesus was a man of power. He knew the strength of stories, gestures and poetic images. He knew how to be a powerful teacher in the way he dealt with people. The sheer impact of this teacher on the history of the world shows what magic he had. So it makes sense to me that early on magi from the East came not just to show him honor, but to connect with him as one of them.

Personally, as someone who wants to develop a fresh spiritual way of life, I include magic as one of the essential elements of my life, along with prayer, contemplation, music, deep reading, nature, the study of spiritual classics, ritual, family life, dedicated work, thoughtful parenting, joyful play, purposeful travel and the serious use of art. Natural magic is a soulful way to be in the world, and it binds together the spiritual and the material in beautiful ways.

I'm fully aware that I'm out of step with my times in my appreciation for the Renaissance natural magic Ficino brought to light—it was around before him, and in fact he borrowed heavily from Muslim scholars, especially one named Al-Kindi.

In my own life, the magic of Christmas has gone though some changes. In my childhood Christmas was saturated with the holy and exciting magic of the tree, gifts, food and social gatherings. I was virtually out of my mind with excitement. When I became a father, I remember that my own two children would wake up around four o'clock in the morning on Christmas day to go to the living room and see if Santa had come. They were excited by the magic as well.

Now the magic is calmer and deeper. I love having my family around during the solstice holidays and exchanging gifts that are full of deep sensitivity for the other person's inclinations and desires. What a good model for the world community!

But back to the meaning of magic. Most of all, it is a way of having real impact on life in everyday situations. A magus is a person who seeks special powers that are natural but often overlooked and unused. He may try to create a language or images that move people or make them feel better. He might compose or play music that heals. One example of natural magic today would be the advertising copywriter in search of a slogan or picture that will compel people to buy his product (magic is not always lofty in its aims). An ambitious preacher might try to convert souls through the dramatic presentation of his message. Parents may look for just the right word to quiet their children. All of this is magic, not very rational but entirely natural.

The magus of the past sometimes described his efforts as tapping into neglected and unknown powers in nature in order to make life better and to be more effective. I once had a remarkable conversation with the highly accomplished and talented Andrew Young, who had been a close companion of Dr. Martin Luther King Jr. as well as ambassador to the UN and mayor of Atlanta. He told me that when he was an ambassador, he accomplished more by playing tennis with leaders from around the world than by being "on the job." This is certainly a magus at work.

Marsilio Ficino found magic in music and used it for healing, especially for psychological disturbances. He grounded his magic in astrology, forever pointing out that doing things at exactly the right time according to the rhythms of nature gave them extra power. He'd keep his eye on the moon and never started a big project when the moon was waning. He also recommended using certain spices, sounds, aromas and colors for maximum effect.

We could all employ the magic of cooking, designing and decorating our homes and workplaces, along with arts like singing and painting, to have more power in life. Gardening, too, has long been a form of magic, creating a natural space that can be calming, encouraging, and reflective.

Today the phrase "magical thinking" refers to a negative condition in which a person may become anxious, fearing that his thoughts will have disastrous consequences in the world. This is not the kind of magic I'm referring to. I'm describing a positive, healthy alternative to the high rational thinking that characterizes our time.

John Dee, later a highly effective magus who studied Ficino and counseled Queen Elizabeth I and her explorers and navigators, believed that he could receive the guidance of angels by using an obsidian mirror. This may seem absurd to a modern person, but the shiny stone has been used that way in many parts of the world.

Robert Fludd was an alchemist, too, but focused on the power of music to reveal the laws of nature and to make nature's secret powers available to the human being willing to go far past the usual channels and methods. He often apportioned experiences to body, soul and spirit, looking to the planets for soul and to the angels for spirit.

Most magi thought highly of astrology and wanted their efforts to be in tune with the timing of the seasons and the movements of the planets. This is the sort of magus who, according to the Gospel nativity story, got on a camel and followed the star to Bethlehem to honor the greatest of all the magi, the Christos himself.

Jesus was a complicated figure, in the best sense, and he shows many faces, including the face of the magus, the healer, the storyteller, and the prophet—that is, the one who speaks for the sky spirit and helps people see their blindness. Changing water to wine, healing at a distance, and rising from death are acts that any magus would envy. And neither to the magus nor for Jesus are these actions a showman's trickery; rather, they are an indication of a compassionate bodhisattva's power from above.

When we hear that magi traveled to honor Jesus after his birth, we can't help but think deeply about the mystery of who Jesus was. He could heal and persuade and charm people with his stories and careful use of language and gesture. Was there ever anyone in history so effective with the tools of the magus, who always sought the most simple means to create the greatest effect?

In their modernism and religious piety, some may take offense at referring to Jesus as a magus. But throughout history the magus has been a person of extensive education, wisdom, and holiness. John Dee was said to have perhaps the best library in Europe in his time, and he was associated with both Oxford and Cambridge universities. Ficino was a priest, a translator, an interpreter of Greek philosophy, and a highly sensitive soul.

Christmas is also a time of real magic. I will never get over the experience as a young child of coming into the living room in our very modest working-class house and seeing the tree shining with its lights and ornaments, gifts surrounding the base of the tree and people much cheerier than normal. Grandparents, uncles and aunts, and friends of the family would come over and be in a festive mood and bring even more gifts. I didn't notice that a bicycle that appeared one Christmas morning was the same one my young uncle rode for years, now freshly painted and completely rehabilitated.

To me this was all magic, the work of Santa and his helpers. The whole thing cast a spell on me, and I didn't want the day to end. Is this experience of Christmas magic a commercialization of the festival? I don't think so. It's the fullness of the experience, the magic that Jesus knew could happen if we viewed life differently and lived accordingly. For me the bounty of Christmas dovetailed with the holiness of the evening Mass and the stories of the child's birth. I observed my mother and father's reverence for the feast as it linked seamlessly with their joy in celebration, especially with me and the other children.

It's simple logic: The magi are central figures in the story of Jesus's birth, and so the magic of Christmas is entirely appropriate. Whatever brings out the magic of the season is in full accord with the theology of the festival, and that includes many aspects that some consider secular. The air of magic around the Christmas tree contributes to and doesn't necessarily take away from the central mystery of new life that is the root meaning of Christmas.

Of course, people can get carried away with food and drink and spend too much money on gifts and be anxious about many aspects of the celebration. But anything, even good things, can be carried too far. You can get so wrapped up in your church and your theological and moral concerns that you lose touch with your humanity, and that indeed is a tragedy. You can overdo Christmas or take it in the wrong way, but that doesn't mean that the magic of the season is false.

TRAVELERS FROM THE EAST

The Magi came from the East to find the anointed child. (When I use the word *anointed*, keep in mind Christos and the anointed lettuce that becomes salad.) The Greek word used for the East is *anatole*, which means sunrise. So even in that word we have an astrological reference, in the larger sense of attending to whatever is going on in the sky. They came from the place of the sunrise and kept their eyes on the night sky and a special star. They were magi who knew that life can be well-guided by signs and portents. They were not rationalists but understood the intelligence of symbols and omens.

How interesting that in this birth narrative, often understood only in Judeo-Christian terms, these foreign astrologers and practitioners of magic would come as the first visitors to the infant born on that holy night. From the beginning it appears that the message of Jesus was intended for everyone, not just those in his religious circle.

They traveled from afar, knowing that he was worthy of worship, just as today some people travel philosophically a great distance to honor the Christos.

It's wonderful to be proud of your Christian inheritance and allegiance, but you can be too proud and not heed the many signs in the stories about Jesus that point to the important and beautiful role of the foreigner, the one who is not a believer but who will make an arduous pilgrimage to offer gifts. The stranger may be able to appreciate the event more than the local.

There was no room in the inn, the angels wished peace to people who are pleasing to the heavens, and then the magi come from where the sun rises. All of these references suggest that Christmas is for everyone, not the chosen few and not a small circle. No one is outside the circle of those huddled around the small barn and the manger and the baby.

The magi are Anatolians, people from where the sun rises. Today we might use the word *oriental* but we refer to a land even farther away. Maybe we should be more interested, in view of the magi, in how this festival and its message are received in India, China, Japan, Korea, and Indonesia. We could even see it linking with the fascinating tradition that Jesus lived in India and studied with theologians from there. You don't have to take that legend as literal history in order to expand your imagination about who and what Jesus was. Just entertaining the possibility with an open mind and curious heart is enough.

If you were to elaborate on the story of the magi, you might imagine that they have a role in the story because

Jesus visited them and studied with them and was a magus himself. In that regard, there is a striking tradition that Jesus was tattooed because of his connection with Egyptian wisdom. None of these narrative elements are firmly historical, but they surround Jesus with a rich imagination, just as the magi do, who make their journey from the East—a place full of fantasy.

It's a mysterious part of the Christmas story: Astrologers from a distant land notice signs of a big event, maybe even the birth of a major spiritual figure, and they make the journey to give to the infant gifts of gold, frankincense, and myrrh. Gold is fairly simple: a valuable gift in any era. Frankincense is also understandable, especially in a day when spices and fragrances were exotic and expensive. Myrrh is similar, but it has the added quality of being used for burial. As you read the Gospels, you come across several foreshadowings of Jesus's death. Myrrh appears later when, after the execution, Joseph of Arimathea, later a major figure in the Grail Legend, supplies myrrh for preparing the body for internment.

T.S. Eliot notes this connection with death in his famous poem "Journey of the Magi." The poet seems to see—at least in the character who speaks the poem, one of the magi—the end of the pagan era with its magic and astrology. But could the hint of death also address the tragedy that the Jesus vision never really took hold in the culture? We still live the old way, on principles that he thought were archaic and self-destructive. We still judge most things by their financial worth. We still aim for power and position. We still fight wars with our neighbors. We still think it's foolhardy to love your enemies. For all the promise of Christmas, there is the sad shadowy realization that the birth led to death and failure.

If you think that Christmas is about an emotional faith in the person of Jesus or a church institution, you may not see failure. But if you understand Jesus's vision as the forming of a worldwide loving community, then you have the painful realization that we are far from that utopia. The Christmas tree is also the tree of Golgotha, the place of crucifixion.

Still, we are left with hope and with a season of good cheer, family love and gift-giving—foretellings of a new dispensation. This kind of hope is of great value, but it is tinged with the sadness of unrealized promise. We still have the Jesus vision, and many individuals and small communities do their best to live it out. But we have not created a new kingdom of love. Not yet.

Maybe to fully appreciate Christmas we have to see its shadow. For all the good cheer, we have a world in trouble, precisely because it doesn't recognize the intelligence and applicability of Jesus's vision. We come to see a birth, but we also witness death. Christmas Day is a time of merry wishes, but it also contains the strains of a later Good Friday in Jerusalem and the rejection of what was promised in Bethlehem. Christmas is bittersweet, the living out of the Jesus vision for humanity and the unspoken awareness that his vision is not yet fully a reality.

CHAPTER TEN

Gift-Giving as a Way of Life

I begin my Christmas shopping in late summer when I have no pressure from a fast-approaching holiday. Especially when I'm traveling, I like to find gifts that are unique, show some craft, express some spiritual theme, and relate both to me and to my loved one. I also look for toys and games, because for me Christmas is always about play and fun. The old festivals of Saturnalia, coinciding with Christmas, included gift-giving and toys, so on this point I have an ancient tradition behind me.

How to Give Gifts

Many people feel anxiety around the gift-giving of the holiday. Will he like my gift? Is it too expensive, not expensive enough? Is it appropriate? Gift-giving clearly involves risks, and the exchange of gifts may be the occasion of sensitive worry on the part of both the giver and the receiver. Notice how much is going through the minds of both when they offer and open gifts. Any object may be loaded with fantasy—especially those gifts that bear an unspoken message or weigh the importance of the relationship.

Gift-giving requires reflection, along with some fantasy about the person who will receive our gift. We have to think carefully about that person to assess the right gift for the right time and occasion. The process of finding a good gift stirs the heart and may open it up, if the search for a gift is real and not just an obligation. When deep reflection and risk-taking go out of the process of finding a good gift, the financial value may take over, and then gift-giving may feel like a burden and deplete our energy.

In his signature book *The Gift*, Lewis Hyde tells an intriguing story about Christmas gifts: "I had a friend in college who once decided to stop participating in the family celebration of Christmas. He explained himself in several ways—the great distance to travel, the waste of money, the commercialization of the holiday—but whatever the reason, his absence removed him from a gift ceremony that would have reaffirmed his connection to family at exactly the time when he wanted to leave it. (The same friend rejoined the family Christmas in later years, the group spirit of a gift holiday being less threatening once he had established his own identity.)"[6]

There may be serious consequences to giving and receiving gifts. A person gives you a nice gift and you may feel beholden to him, no longer as free as you used to be. As in Lewis Hyde's example, the process of exchanging gifts places you in a gift community and it may do so covertly. You may not be aware of the implications of participating. In my family, I noticed that the first Christmas my daughter's husband joined us and participated in the gift exchange, he took a deeper step into the family. The gifts were a form of welcoming and a more serious inclusion.

Around the Christmas tree there may be a huge flurry of emotions and hidden thoughts about the gifts. Watch people exchanging gifts, and you will see how deeply and sometimes how desperately they're thinking. Gifts are not a simple thing. If they are not exactly commensurate with the quality of the relationship, they could embarrass or disappoint. If the gift is too elaborate or expensive, it's difficult to accept gracefully. If it's less than one's expectations, it may cause anxious concentration.

WHY GIFTS AT CHRISTMAS?

In the larger context of Christmas and its deep universal theology that I am presenting here, gifts are particularly expressive. The magi thought to bring valuable gifts to the child Jesus, and those gifts were symbolic. Most gifts are. Gold to the king of a new kind of kingdom, frankincense to man who would be an Epicurean in love with life, and myrrh to the man who would be executed for his generous audacity.

Why would these wise men bring such gifts to a child? Because they had spent their lives, presumably, in search for wisdom and insight, for methods that they could trust and use effectively. These occult methods, strange to the average person, gave them hidden knowledge, including the revelation that a person had been born who might save the world from its insanity. They brought gifts to support and further the promise of this child and the revolution he stood for. The gifts said: "We are with you. We appreciate who you are and what you have to do. We have seen the signs and believe that they are reliable. We have made an arduous journey just to see you and feed our hope. We want you to thrive and be successful."

As a parent at Christmas I have a similar sentiment. I want my children to know that I love them and appreciate them. I see the Christos in them. I see the future of the human race. I hope that they can bring it out of its ignorance and immaturity. I didn't travel miles to see them, but I do want to give them support. I believe in them, and I hope my gifts will tell them that I love them and stand by them.

Think of the complicated emotions and fantasies you have as you unwrap a gift. You have value. Someone has thought about you and wants to make you happy. With all the challenges in life, at this moment you are tasting life's capacity to give you not only what you need but what you desire.

In a world largely dedicated to a "quid pro quo" economy—even in our relationships—we expect to get what we need only by putting in our time at work or first giving another person what he needs: then I'll get what I want. In this context, a gift stands out. The heart appears. There is no demand but only positive regard.

People complain that gift-giving becomes empty, frenetic, and annoying. But the problem may not be the giving of gifts but the way we do it. The basic principle is: Anything you do without soul will feel empty and meaningless. So, the task at Christmas is to approach gifts in a different way, in a way that will have some depth and emotion.

Giving with Soul

Knowing the deeper importance of Christmas and the role of gifts in the philosophy and values of the festival might help keep gift-giving joyous and meaningful. How you imagine gifts makes all the difference. But you have to educate, train and practice a deeper way of giving.

First, don't think of gifts in the usual way, as just something you want to do for people close to you, or worse, an obligation demanded by Christmas custom and family tradition. Think of a gift as the language of your soul. With your gift, as simple as it may be, you want to say something to the person receiving it, and that message is precise and particular. It's more than generic love and good wishes. As you search for or make your gift, you could fill it with your fantasies of good will.

Christmas gifts represent the evolved way of life Jesus recommended for humanity as a whole. You live from the heart, you tame your ego cravings (that's the meaning, in part, of the Gospel practicing of getting rid of negative urges), and you foster community and connection over self-interest. Gift-giving with purity of heart represents the Jesus way; it is more about community than about a personal attempt to be loved or reciprocated. The family around the tree, at least for this day, represents the world living by the joyous principle of love rather than by competition and rules.

Christmas gifts are a taste of utopia, a way of being in the world that flows from the heart and overcomes ego anxieties. In this way, gifts are the real meaning of Christmas and are an important part of the entire, multifaceted festival. If Christmas is about creating a liminal world, separate from the one we know too well, then gift-giving is the central act of that world.

Knowing this, you might put your heart into the gifts instead of being half-hearted with them. You could appreciate Christmas, as it was centuries ago, as a time-out from life as usual. Take it as a break from the extreme focus on money and possessions that is so central in modern life and from the usual economics of life. For one day at least, Christmas is a gift culture, an aspect of our utopian purpose.

If your intention with gifts is to make a better world, in deep alignment with the Jesus teaching and many other spiritual traditions of enlightenment, you may not feel burned-out by the obligations and activities of the season. You may look forward to giving gifts as a way of ritually making a step forward in evolution. You may use your imagination more fully, understanding the inherent importance of gifts. You could enter gift-giving as a new way of life, as an aspect of a joyous worldview free of narcissism. Whenever we make anything too personal instead of communal, it becomes a burden. And, if you don't have an expansive philosophy of Christmas, you may reduce it to money and things and celebrations that have little substance beyond self-interest.

The Magi who came from the place of the rising sun understood the power of magic, and for that reason they brought meaningful and beautiful gifts to the child. The gifts were a kind of magic, as our Christmas gifts can be. They can help create a better life for all children and for others by evoking the power of love and community. The special enchanting spirit of Christmas is crucial to the festival, and gifts can intensify that spirit.

Jesus himself seems to have lived in a gift economy of sorts. Maybe he was a carpenter, but the stories of his life depict a teacher and healer who is supported by the people around him. He is generous, as we see in the stories where he miraculously conjures up fish sandwiches to feed thousands of people listening to his teaching, and when he heals people suffering from various illnesses. He is both a good giver and a good receiver.

Anthropology and philosophy delve into the complexities and shadow aspects of gifts and the idea of a gift economy. For our purposes, we may reflect on the utopian ideals of the Jesus way and give gifts at Christmas in that spirit, without being discouraged by the dark aspects of gift-giving: doing it out of proportion, anxiously, with the expectation of getting something in return.

In many instances it's as difficult, or more difficult, to receive a gift than to give one. You are willing to show some dependence, which is not in itself a bad thing. You may even say, perhaps nonverbally, that you are in need.

What I enjoy most about receiving gifts is seeing how another person, usually someone I love, is thinking about me and wants to care for me. This is a dance of relationship, and my part is to receive the gift gracefully. In some ways it takes more strength of character to receive than to give a gift. But both sides of this heart-skill are necessary to establish a community that is not focused on amassing personal possessions—the darker side of money.

Jesus tells that strange story of the people who work in a vineyard: some work all day, some about half a day, and some an hour or so. They all get paid the same. Jesus, that infant in the crib, offers a different fantasy of economics, and his entire approach is based on the primacy of the heart.

The color of the heart is red, for obvious reasons. Notice Santa's red suit, strings of red beads on the tree, as well as many red ornaments, red napkins and place-mats, red dresses and ties at parties. The primacy of the heart. The gift economy of the heart stands in on this one day for the usual economy of hours worked, seniority, rank, productivity and advancement. Christmas is not just a holiday; it's the microcosm of what a renewed life might look like, at least in principle.

GIVING FROM THE HEART

If you have lost sight of the deep role of gift-giving at Christmas, wrap your presents in red, just to remind you of the heart. Give a gift that is meaningful to you and to the one receiving it. Embrace the giving and heart-centered spirit of Christmas, and don't try to justify it through some abstract point of theology. Giving is the active theology appropriate to the festival.

In my world, the gift economy applies to every aspect of my life and work, but it isn't usually plain, obvious and uncomplicated. Often, when I travel to speak for a group, I will give a free talk at a church or hospice. I will charge less than my usual fee. I will make a special effort to be available to people by spending extra time with them. Whenever I sign books, I do it slowly, offering a small conversation to anyone who wants one. This is a portioned gift economy that has the advantage of not standing out as a radical experiment but only as a tweaking of the usual, introducing the gift economy in single strands, like threads of gold leaf in a fabric of dark cotton.

In speaking of gifts, the highly imaginative cultural philosopher Ivan Illich once said that the Christian churches make a mistake in institutionalizing the gift of caring for people in need, when it would be much more beneficial for individual people inspired by the Jesus way to make "gifting" part of their personal lives. Institutional aid is valuable and can be full of heart, but if it takes away from a personal lifestyle of giving, the loss is significant.

Gifts are an expression of the heart, as is the core of the Jesus philosophy, where the well-known Greek word *agape* is key. The word refers to a kind of love that is like that of husband and wife, not just momentarily passionate but steady, ongoing affection and dedication to a life together. Agape is sometimes like brotherhood and community, and it can also be an appreciation for things. In the ancient world, the loving goddess Isis was referred to as the "Agape Goddess" and was pictured much like a Madonna caring for her child.

This is the deeper spirit behind a serious effort to give gifts and to make gifting a way of life. You can do this simply and with pleasure in your daily interactions. Instead of basing them entirely on a paid-for-services model, you can add gifts where appropriate—but always gifts that have some heart in them. It isn't enough to create a business program that looks like gift-giving but lacks a real heart.

Christmas gift-giving is a ritual that expresses the idea in the hothouse of the Christmas season but serves as a model for the rest of the year. If Christmas giving is genuine and generous, then maybe life during the year will have the qualities of this aspect of Christmas, qualities that can help us evolve into more humane and loving people.

CHAPTER ELEVEN

Santa, the Holy One

With the emphasis at Christmas on the sky, it isn't so surprising that the holiday should have led to a grandfather figure like Santa Claus who streaks across the heavens in his sleigh. He pilots his reindeer around the world, the ultimate gift-giver and embodiment of generosity, good cheer, and love of children. It's also remarkable that he has become the last living mythic figure to be treated as almost real by a society that has worked consciously to eradicate myth. What other figure of the imaginal realm has remained so alive in the imaginations of both children and adults?

Santa, I know, may seem light, commercial, and pagan: a figure for children but not for adults trying to make solid sense of this important festival. But hear me out.

THE REAL SANTA

If you know any Romance languages or have traveled, you've come across the word *santa* many times. Santa Barbara, Santa Maria, Santa Lucia, San Francisco. Santa means "holy" or "holy one." There in the name is a hint, not just about the origins of his name in St. Nicholas but also about his nature. He's not just a goblin; he's a saint, the object of religious awe and honor. What if we treated him like a saint as much as a gnome?

He's a holy figure, and yet I don't want to take the fun away from him and make him into a humorless saint. After all, his jovial spirit and sense of generosity are precisely what make him holy. But if we lose the "Santa" in Santa Claus, I fear we'll reduce him to a fairy-tale figure rather than a serious representative of the evolved human being the Christmas story is all about.

I want to restore a deep appreciation for Santa and the values he represents—happiness, joviality, generosity, and kindness. These are the very qualities central to the new world envisioned in the Gospels. Jesus was the one who advocated a life of agape, of love and affection, rather than rules and authorities. Accordingly, Santa is a non-authoritarian elder, a man of golden character who also appreciates fun and games and children. When Jesus says, "Let the little children come to me," he is making way for Santa. In fact, at that moment in the Gospel story, Jesus looks like Santa.

Santa lives at the North Pole, a special liminal place, a kind of utopian nowhere. He lives outside of normal human life and takes his meaning from that nowhere place. There the veil is thin, as the popular saying goes, and enchanting things happen. There you are not bound by the limits of natural law. Reindeer fly, a sleigh holds a worldful of Christmas presents, and billions of letters are read and answered. It's a realm run on the principles of magic and miracle.

Santa embodies a special spirit that is cheerful, kind, open to children, and above all generous. But Jesus is also a holy one, kind, open to children and generous.

He too is cheerful, although that aspect didn't make it into the accepted versions of the Gospel. In the so-called Gnostic Gospels, Jesus laughs at and with his students. The profound and yet very human story of his first miracle, at the wedding party in Cana, also shows a warm and caring Jesus, someone who is not above offering the ordinary, human gift of wine (setting aside the important symbolism of the story) when it has run out.

Santa brings happiness to the world through gifts. He has rosy cheeks and, though a saint, he is not gaunt and ascetic in appearance. He loves life. His key expression is a laugh: "Ho, ho, ho!" Notice the ritual aspects of these qualities.

SACRED QUALITIES OF SANTA

"Ho, ho, ho," understood widely as the language and vocabulary of Santa, is his mantra—ritual words that express his being and his power. In some religions, a mantra is a word or words that, sounded thoughtfully, can make any action sacred. A person who is initiated into a special spiritual role may be given a special mantra to use throughout his or her life. These are words used to sanctify rather than to express an idea or a feeling. In this sense, Santa's words, "ho, ho, ho," serve well to manifest his essence and his values. Jesus says, "The kingdom is near." The angel says, "Don't be afraid." Santa says, "Ho, ho, ho."

With his stocking cap, bells, wide girth and cheerful mantra, Santa also has qualities of the holy fool. This is a figure in many spiritual traditions who does silly things and makes people laugh, but his purpose is deadly serious: to help people get away from the heavy, rational burden of a ponderous life. He wants to break through the logical and the practical in a funny way, using gentle humor as a means to the holy. This role is particularly fitting because Christmas comes during the gap between darkness and sunlight—the perfect time, traditionally, to stop being normal and to begin experimenting with alternative ways.

What about those bells that Santa wears? For one thing, they emphasize the shaman side of Santa. Shamans might wear or use rattles that are either like bells or are bells. They announce the presence of the shaman or the evocation of spirits. They protect the shaman and those he is healing. They may be used to summon a spirit or to make the realm of spirit accessible and open. They can sanctify a space or play a role in healing, perhaps opening the person to the influence of a spirit.

Santa's bells announce the presence of someone from another dimension. You hear the bells and you are ready to suspend your disbelief and open up your imagination. Santa's bells are similar to the ones I would ring as an altar boy during the solemn moment when bread, according to belief, became the body of Christ: a liminal breakthrough in the Catholic Mass. Sometimes these bells are chimes, but sometimes jingling bells, just like Santa's, and for a similar purpose.

It's a small, almost insignificant signal, this jingle of bells, but the realm of the sky almost always announces itself quietly and gently. Nothing overdone. Extreme subtlety. I once observed a shaman teaching his students how to use his bell-like rattle to break through to the other world. I can imagine Santa teaching his elves exactly how to wear the jingles so they can do their magic.

All of these qualities together make Santa a good image for Christmas. He has the solstice liminal qualities: the joy of new light, the inversion of normal values and customs, an otherworldly costume, a recognizable mantra. At the same time, he embodies the Jesus values of generosity and care. In other words, he blends the two basic ingredients of Christmas: solstice liminality with the Jesus utopian vision for humankind.

SANTA AS SHAMAN

Santa is more shaman than priest, because he can feel at home in both the heavens and on earth. Like a shaman, he flies through the sky and brings benefits for people in their homes. Shamans usually move in two directions: outward toward the realm of spirit and then back to community. Santa goes off on his sleigh and otherwise is either in his home at the North Pole or in other people's homes. He moves between the worldwide sky and the intimate home. To him, travel and home are both central. Like Jesus, who often stays in the homes of his friends and then addresses his father above, Santa is both intimate and visionary.

Santa is at home on the earth and in the sky, and he uses music—remember the carols of Christmas—for healing and magic. While the shaman favors the drum and bells, Santa is associated with Christmas carols and that special group of musicians who stand on street corners and outside homes, caroling. People gathering to sing carols are performing yet another of the essential rituals of Christmas, emphasizing community, good cheer and the enchantment of certain songs that have become part of the festival. I use the word *ritual* in this context with considerable weight and precision. From the Santa perspective, caroling is serious business.

If we think of Santa as a shaman, a spiritual leader who has the skills needed to enter a reality different from the usual for the benefit of his or her community, then to give Santa a welcome at Christmas is to invite healing. The real shaman is a spiritual healer who gets to the roots of a person's problems. He heals one's attitude toward life and resets the focus on love and community.

Santa's reindeer flight, his home at the North Pole, and his tendency to be heard on rooftops all suggest, in a child-like and folk-hearted way, shamanic abilities. Shamans can do things that normal humans only dream about. They know the future, they heal at a distance, and they promote a deeply communal approach to everyday life. They also communicate at a distance and travel by magic.

Santa's relationship with children is another aspect of his "spirituality." The way Santa is portrayed, there seems to be a special understanding between him and children. In this he is akin to the so-called "laughing Buddha" who sometimes is shown with children climbing all over him and with a sack of gifts.

Santa is also associated with the fireplace or hearth and, in fact, enters the home through the chimney, in a magical descent that is a kind of incarnation and a Gnostic "fall" into the human condition. As above, so below. This, too, is an essential aspect of Christmas. It is all about the union of the realm above with this world below, angels in the heavens and Jesus in the manger. Like Jesus, Santa comes down to our lowly realm and leaves his gifts. We listen for sounds on the roof (the upper realm) and then see signs of his having descended. Leaving cookies and milk for Santa and then finding them eaten is still another small but important ritual expressing the magic and liminality of Christmas Eve.

Santa is earthy, jovial, and quite human, though he is also fantastic and magical. There is a pagan side to Santa. Unfortunately, Christians have not appreciated the pagan spirits and have fought them for centuries. Yet the pagan spiritual figures are also holy and important.

Santa wears red. There are many symbolic reds: the red of anger, the red of fire, and the red of blood, vitality. This is Santa, red with an enthusiasm for life and a joyous, sanguine spirit. The red clothes go with his rosy cheeks and cheery spirit. As we have seen, they represent the great heart that lies at the center of the Christmas festival.

Santa's white, silvery full beard gives him some age. You couldn't imagine Santa in his thirties, and yet he isn't a typical elder. He is more like a grandfather than a father, but he's quite agile on the roof and in guiding his sleigh. Imagine him through the archetypal image of the "Good Grandfather"— kindly, generous and jovial.

THE IMPORTANCE OF SANTA

It's too bad that we have to grow up and away from our "belief" in Santa, with all its vivid imagination and unbounded kindness. We are left with a much cooler, darker, more dangerous world, one that is on its own, without the assuring presence of a holy one who lives at the North Pole ready to give us what we need. We think we mature and grow out of naive belief when we stop believing in Santa, but it would be more appropriate to say that we lose our sense of enchantment and the magic of what it means to be human.

Imagine if we simply translated the name Santa into our own language, saying in English "Holy One." We might have a different understanding of Christmas and gift-giving and partying. We might restore a sense of the holy to Santa, or at least a degree of seriousness and gravity. What if "The Holy One" visited our home and left us gifts? What if "The Holy One" gave gifts to children all over the world? This new sense of Santa might inspire us to bring the spirit of Christmas into our world.

For me, Santa is a deep expression of the true meaning of Christmas. It's a meaning that could inspire anyone of any spiritual faith or of no particular faith. It could give us more reason to do special things for this festival, especially to open our hearts in kindness and generosity.

Generosity is a special virtue that is often overlooked. Santa models it. Who else gives wonderful gifts to every child on the planet? Who else thinks so highly of children as to dedicate his life to them? Who else links arms with parents to improve the lives of children? What other spiritual figure is known primarily for his rosy cheeks and jovial laugh?

In the spirit of Santa and of trying to make the most of the spirituality of Christmas, as I mentioned, I always buy a toy for my children, no matter how old they are. By now they expect a toy from me, sometimes a board game that the family can play together and sometimes an outdoor gadget that will get us playing.

Santa reminds us that play and fun are essential to a meaningful life. Let me give you a little piece of psychological logic that I like to use. If our lives are only serious and lack sufficient fun and play, then our seriousness is probably a defense against play and not fully real in itself. Our seriousness would improve and deepen if we allowed more play in life. The opposite is also true: If we are not serious about life, then our playing is probably superficial —mere entertainment when it should be the source of deep joy.

I recommend that we restore the true meaning of Christmas: good gift-giving, fun and play, great food, and family gatherings. If you look closely at the Gospel stories and teachings, you will find a similar if not identical philosophy. The best way to celebrate Christmas, if the emphasis is on Christ, is to live out the spirit of those teachings and example. If your preference is to focus on the natural symbols of the solstice, then this is also a time of unusual generosity and fun.

CHAPTER TWELVE

The Birth of the Soul

y favorites among the many extraordinary paintings of annunciation—the moment when Mary mysteriously becomes pregnant by a holy spirit—are two by the Italian Renaissance artist Sandro Botticelli. The one painted in 1485 delicately shows a parallel between the soft and gossamer wings of the angel and Mary's halo, while it also places a heavy architectural barrier between the angel and the human. The angel holds a lily honoring Mary's virginity, and they bow to each other, representatives of two separate realms acknowledging each other—spirit and flesh, this world and other world.

The later 1490 painting is bolder and heavier, and it shows a very different scene. Now there is only a slight window line in the background to separate the two realms, and there is no longer the feeling of equality and reciprocity. The Virgin Mary pushes her arms out and sways her body back as if to pull away from the angel's message.

I have always been drawn to the later painting because of the beautiful gesture of resistance on the part of Mary, but now I favor the earlier one for its delicacy and its way of mirroring the high realm of spirit with the lower realm of earthly life. In any case, we are dealing with perhaps the greatest mystery in all of human experience: the meeting of the exalted spiritual world with an ordinary person. At the deepest level this is what Christmas is all about, and although we have already treated aspects of this great mystery, it's time now to deal with it head on.

INCARNATION

Once again I remind myself that I want to write for Christians and those who are not Christian, in fact those who have no allegiance to any system of faith and belief. Let's see if we can follow this highly theological idea of incarnation, the spiritual becoming human, without any need for belief or acceptance of a Christian point of view. For Christians, I want to deepen this essential theological idea in livable, ordinary terms. This is all quite a challenge.

We have several extraordinary images: the angel and Mary representing two vastly separate worlds almost touching each other. Think of the celebrated image of the Sistine Chapel where God's finger just about comes into contact with Adam's. Then there are the shepherds in the fields standing in the glow of a host of angels honoring the birth. Shepherds and angels, earth and sky.

In the story of the annunciation, the angel Gabriel informs Mary that her child will be called "son of the highest." So, once again the highest realm meets with lowly humanity to create a human being who is the issue of both. When the child is born and glorious angels appear and simple shepherds stand in awe, the union of the high and low is complete.

Christmas shows that it's possible for a human being to be at the highest level possible and yet remain deeply human at the same time. The Gospels portray a Jesus who is supremely compassionate and capable of love and friendship, who loves food and uses his wit, and at the same time is forever aware that he has a father in the sky, a father at the highest level far beyond the human.

All of this may seem interesting or irrelevant. To me personally, it's the key to how my life has come together. I've always had intimations of a vaster world in which human life plays out. I remember becoming an altar boy at our small church in Detroit in the late 1940s. My first task was to stay after school and practice reciting the Latin prayers. I still remember holding the pamphlets and cards on which the prayers were printed, Latin in red, and feeling like I was knocking on the doors of the highest places, by which I mean high above the clouds.

At Mass and during the celebration of other sacraments, I could sense the otherworld conjured by the beeswax and candle flames, the incense, and the silky robes of the priests. Above all, I felt the solemn event of the trans-formation of bread into the body of Christ as a sacred moment. Later, whenever I saw the red glassed-in candle glowing in a darkened sanctuary, instinctively I responded with deep reverence, as I do today.

I began my life learning how to detect the absolutely holy in a place made for a profound spiritual experience. I understand that if you haven't been brought up this way you may not feel what I feel. What I sense as supremely holy may be only a symbol to you. But you probably have your own ways to bring the sacred into your life. It could be a mountain or a lake or revered farmland. The point is that the things of nature and the world can embody the most sacred reality imaginable.

All of this the theologians call *incarnation*, as in "carnal," which leads me to a very different kind of Christmas message in the Gospel of John, who doesn't tell the familiar Christmas story of the birth at Bethlehem. Here's what John says:

> In the beginning there was the logos.
> And the logos was in the company of God.
> God was the logos.
> It was in the pre-dawn with God.
> Through it everything came to be.
> Without it nothing that is would have come to be.
> In it there was the spark of life,
> and that life was the light of humanity.
> The light shines in the darkness
> and the darkness doesn't darken it....
> The logos became flesh and lived with us.
> We saw and appreciated his brilliance,
> the brilliance of one who is the only child of the
>   father,
> full of grace and depth. (John 1:1-5, 14)

This is very mysterious language for what happened and happens at Christmas. The very meaning of life gets a body and a human life. The logic of the universe has now become a human being whose purpose is to teach how any of us can also embody that basic meaningfulness.

Forgive my confusing and high spiritual language. I have to say it this way first and then try to make more ordinary sense of it. After all, Jesus was a human child. That's the great mystery discussed by theologians for centuries. How does the great cosmic scheme of the universe take form as a child? How can Christmas make any sense? And when it does finally make sense, how do I take its lessons and become like that child myself? How can I incarnate in my own being the spirit of the most high?

Don't imagine this incarnation of spirit in our lives as a sudden "zap" turning us into angels. Rather, it's a life-long process of impregnating our daily lives with spiritual values based on a transcendent vision.

As I was learning the Latin prayers to be an altar boy, I was being infused with a spirituality that would grow and deepen as I got older. It was only a few years later that I decided to leave home to study for the priesthood —a second big step toward a spiritual identity. I now see my decision to leave the monastery at twenty-six as another decision that furthered the incarnation of a spiritual destiny in my simple life. I was the son of a plumber on my way to discovering what it means to care for your soul. In my twenties I was quite unconscious, just trying to make my way, looking for a life work and a way to stay alive. But a life work has always been at the core of my spirituality. That search, however mundane, like that of ordinary shepherds in a field, was my path toward the logos, the ultimate meaning.

Every major turn was a kind of Christmas. Something was being born, something not entirely material and physical. My destiny was taking flesh step by step.

Today, when I celebrate Christmas, I honor all the people who helped me become intelligent and enlightened enough to find my path, to do more than simply follow my physical cravings and to become a person with one foot on the earth and the other in the heavens. The same can happen to you, if you stretch beyond familial, cultural, and general unconsciousness and eventually discover a meaningful existence.

We often think that we are human beings in search of a spiritual life, but we are also, maybe mostly, spirits looking for persons in whom we can become incarnate. I know, this is similar to Teilhard de Chardin's often quoted statement: "We are not human beings having a spiritual experience. We are spiritual beings having a human experience."

It seems that most people find some level of spiritual fulfillment. They may find it as a parent or spouse or worker. But others apparently succumb to ignorance and unconscious passion in the form of greed, self-advancement, and violence. In those lives the spiritual logos appears to be crowded out. Not that there isn't any hope, but the prospects are slight. Jesus taught this again and again: Not everyone makes it.

THE BIRTH OF THE SOUL

Another way I have pictured the process of incarnating the spiritual in your ordinary life and person is the birth of your soul. John Keats spoke of the appearance of soul as soul-making, and the founder of soul-centered philosophy, Plotinus, said that it's like a sculptor chipping away at stone. The poet Rainer Maria Rilke compared it to bees making honey from flowers. These are all beautiful and appropriate images, but I can also see that our souls are born. There is such a thing as a soulful Christmas.

If the soul is born, that means there is a conception, a period of gestation, and birth. The seeds of my soul are clear: my family. They had warmth, love, struggle, crisis, community, friendship, and hard work in their lives. They loved children and made room for them on every occasion. To be brought up in such an environment is to be given all that is needed for a future soulful life.

For me the pregnancy has been long. Maybe the best way for me to think about the birth of my soul is in stages that overlap. Many births and many pregnancies. The births seem to have happened at turning points: marriage, the birth of my daughter, the publication of *Care of the Soul*. Interestingly, these all took place within a year, 1991. I was fifty-one.

This doesn't mean that a number of good things were not happening before those births. The pregnancies were full of good moments and sad ones. But there was no pushing into life like what happened in that one year when I felt my soul was born, revealed, named, and acknowledged. Christmas 1991 was the key celebration of my soul's birth.

Soul is about life, heart, intimacy, connection, revelation, and presentation of your inner life to the world. It is born when it is ready. The pregnancy requires patience and observation and some experimenting. It is not a passive period. In my case it took a long time.

Soul at Christmas Time

The theological emphasis on Christmas is obviously spiritual in nature. People tend to think of humankind being ennobled by the connection to angels and holy spirits.

But the reverse is also important: the spiritual realm can find a home in humanity and on earth. You could say that spirit finds its soul at Christmas, and therefore the interest in gifts and family and food are appropriate because they are so soulful.

The spirituality of Christmas is to be found in the teachings and the emphasis on the divine, while the soul of the season is there in the gifts and good cheer.

Some of my theologian colleagues are more interested in discussing Christology and incarnation and exactly how the human and the godly are connected in Jesus. Others want to focus on solstice rituals and the mysteries of nature. As a spokesperson for the soul, I'm much more interested in Santa Claus, gifts, food, and family customs. The spirit is important: tradition says it feeds the soul. But spirit often goes to extremes in presenting an image of self-importance. The soul stuff, I admit, is common, ordinary, and close to home, but that doesn't make it any less valuable.

The following are some of the soul-oriented activities that have gathered in many places around Christmas: family and friends, gift-giving, gathering around a dinner table, singing carols, reciting traditional Christmas stories and poems, remembering Christmases of the past and people who were present (memory is a key element in a soulful life). Also, decorating your home, especially giving it the radiance of Christmas lights, makes the festival a family and local celebration—further qualities of soul.

Let's think about this custom in some places of stringing lights inside and outside the home. Of course, it relates to the arrival of light at the time of solstice. That theme is always a key underlying factor in Christmas celebrations. Relating to the birth of Jesus, it is a similar celebration of the light of awareness that he offers in his teaching. He referred to himself as the light of the world. "I am the light of the cosmos. Anyone with me won't walk in darkness but will possess the light of life" (John 8:12).

When the shepherds beheld the choir of angels, they were "shining around" in the night atmosphere. Light is everywhere in the Christmas story and pageant. When we light our homes, we are saying that this family is looking for light in life—understanding, a good direction, relief from ignorance and confusion, a guide for the future, a new enlightened society. Light can be full of spirit, but it is also a soulful thing, especially when connected to the home.

Light is a sign of celebration and happiness. We honor the story of Jesus's birth at the time of solstice, the two events completely intertwined, because it represents the birth of the soul. We have a chance to make our world alive with soul and therefore compassionate, friendly, generous, and child-centered—particular virtues of the Christmas festival.

GOD IS BORN

I use the word *God* sparingly. I agree with many spiritual traditions that warn against using such a word too casually or irreverently. Some would say we should avoid it altogether. Often it is used in a completely spiritual context, naming the creator and sustainer of life, however you'd like to define that. But *God* can also be a word for *soul*, the life within every thing and the meaning that gives it all sense and value.

Let me repeat the opening words of John's Gospel that we saw before from my own translation:

> In the beginning there was the logos.
> And the logos was in the company of God.
> God was the logos.
> It was in the pre-dawn with God.
> Through it everything came to be.
> Without it nothing that is would have come to be.
> In it there was the spark of life,
> and that life was the light of humanity.
> The light shines in the darkness
> and the darkness doesn't darken it. (John 1:1–5)

Logos is a mysterious word, and it is central to the story of Jesus and of Christmas. It is so important that I didn't want to translate this word into English but leave it as a special sacred word. It may refer to word, words, stories, myths, meaning, and mystery. If I have to translate it, I use *mystery*.

John speaks of this mystery in which words and meaning are part of the creation of our world as if it were a person. Logos was in the company of God and in it was the spark of life. Light as a spark that gives us our vitality, makes us alive, not just physically but in every way. This, too, is the meaning of Christmas. This logos, which is also the infant in the manger, brings light to the world. It is a source of light, giving us even more reason to light our homes and trees and fill our tables and mantles with candles and little bulbs. Logos is an interior light that shines out from who we are and what we want to bring to the world. All those Christmas lights we see are an attempt to enlighten our world in its obvious condition of moral and emotional darkness.

In our house, the first thing I do as the solstice approaches is find all our Christmas lights, test them, and string them inside and outside the house. I take this job seriously because I know how important images are, and I desperately want our world to find enlightenment. This is a symbolic way, but we need symbols that speak to us without any need for explanation. Christmas lights do this: They shed light on the world and dispel a little darkness, reminding us that our main task in life is to be among those who have the spark of light in them.

Other things I like doing are singing traditional carols; listening to J.S. Bach's "Christmas Oratorio," which is light in sound; reading Dylan Thomas's *A Child's Christmas in Wales,* a sweet story of a family at Christmas; and reading a favorite poem by D.H. Lawrence called "God is Born."

We celebrate Christmas one day of the year, but Christmas is always happening. God is being born, the spark of life. You don't have to translate this insight into a belief. Just know deep inside yourself and inside the things around you that there is a spark of life. That is what we celebrate at Christmas: the light that manifests the life in all things and in ourselves.

The Spirit of Christmas

hristmas is one of the most soulful days of the year. You don't need to be Christian or a follower of Jesus, because the roots of Christmas lie in the natural rhythms of the year, and solstice celebrations are universal. Christmas is a solstice festival with a significant overlay of the story and teachings of Jesus. But his teaching is universal and dovetails beautifully with the spirit of solstice. Jesus offers a vision of utopia, a perfected world. He envisioned a time when we would get over our neuroses, our demonic tendencies, and live in peaceful community.

The celebration of Christmas can be meaningless and maddening, especially if you don't have access to its deep layers of history and symbolism. You may feel frantic looking for gifts, rather than understanding that gift-giving is a way of being in family, friendship, and community, and that Christmas is a time for modeling a utopian gift economy. You may feel that Christmas is a license to eat and drink too much, and yet the idea of transcending ordinary limits has been part of solstice celebrations for hundreds of years. You don't have to go to literal extremes, but you can stretch your personal rules, based on the idea of liminal time, a period of days or weeks set aside to celebrate an important aspect of life. You could aim for a paradoxical "moderate excess."

It would be better to enter the spirit of the liminal rather than fight it. Step outside of ordinary time: be of good cheer, give some real gifts, make some good food, and spend more time than usual with friends and family. The best way to deal with the exhaustion of the holidays is not to withdraw but to enter them thoughtfully.

Sing the carols, knowing that this is the expression of angels, mysterious separate beings who represent the invisible factors that influence all our lives. Decorate a tree, knowing that its symbolism reaches deep. String some lights, appreciating that light is the main theme of the season.

Christmas is a holy time that invites you to reflect on the most important issues in life, especially escaping the darkness of ignorance and arriving at the light of new understanding and possibility. It ritualizes the birth of your soul. Remember that ritual is an ordinary action carried out with special attention to its poetics that has far greater significance than would appear.

For me personally, Christmas has many rich layers: warm memories of my family from childhood; the brilliant, lighted and festive Christmas Mass; carols and other music associated with the season and somehow of the highest quality; and the theology of incarnation—living a spiritual life deep in the ordinary world.

For our lives, incarnation means being focused on the spiritual and the eternal but bringing that focus deep into life. It also means having the capacity to be both carnal and spiritual, in love with life and yet able to connect with the eternal and the divine. This is really the heart of the Christmas theological message: Live in two worlds that overlap but are distinct. Don't be a materialist, but don't sacrifice your ordinary physical life for any spiritual ideal. Be lowly and lofty.

This teaching, like all good theology, is not aimed only at those who dedicate themselves to the Gospel teaching, but to all people, from believers to skeptics. I wish that those who associate Christmas too closely with Christianity would look deep deeper and see the universal symbols and truths contained in the festival. Isn't that why so many people of different backgrounds are drawn to Christmas—because they see the natural symbols and basic realities celebrated at this time of year?

If you take Christmas to heart and get past the anxieties in arranging for gifts and parties, you will rediscover yourself every year at this time and experience a birth in yourself, just like the one so beautifully described in the Gospel stories. It will be a celebration of both the birth of Jesus and the birth of your own soul.

NOTES

1. Norman O. Brown, *Love's Body* (University of California, 1990), 207.
2. Brown, 208.
3. Teilhard de Chardin, *The Future of Man* (New York: Image, 2004), 307.
4. Elizabeth Brient, *Immanence of the Infinite: Hans Blumenberg and the Threshold to Modernity* (Washington, DC: Catholic University of America), 11.
5. Wallace Stevens, *The Necessary Angel: Essays on Reality and the Imagination* (New York: Vintage, 1965), v.
6. Lewis Hyde, *The Gift* (New York: Vintage, 2007), 86–87.